CityStyle

A FIELD GUIDE TO GLOBAL FASHION CAPITALS

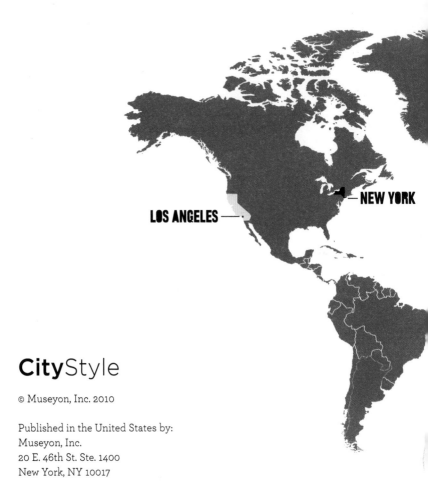

LOS ANGELES ——

—— NEW YORK

CityStyle

© Museyon, Inc. 2010

Published in the United States by:
Museyon, Inc.
20 E. 46th St. Ste. 1400
New York, NY 10017

Museyon is a registered trademark.
Visit us online at www.museyon.com

ISBN 978-0-9822320-7-1

195902

Printed in China

NEW YORK
PARIS
MILAN
LONDON
TOKYO
STOCKHOLM
SYDNEY
LOS ANGELES

FOREWORD

Like it or not, fashion is the one art form we encounter every day. Even those who choose to ignore fashion's whims make a statement with everything they wear. All over the world, our clothing says something about who we are in the local visual language. It tells others what we value, which social groups we belong to, and how we perceive ourselves. And those symbols change from city to city.

Fashion is of-the-moment by its very nature. It is often the first of the arts to reflect and react to shifts in the world around us. Hemlines rise and fall, military looks replace frivolous glamour, and the style cycle goes round.

From prestigious couturiers to exciting new voices, this book offers a snapshot of contemporary style in eight fashion capitals around the globe—some established, some emerging and some on the decline. Together, these essays and interviews present of a slice of urban life as we live it today.

CityStyle

NEW YORK 10

PARIS 46

TOKYO 144

STOCKHOLM 176

MILAN 82

LONDON 112

SYDNEY 202

LOS ANGELES 232

CONTRIBUTORS

PARIS, p.48

Lauren Drablier grew up in Egypt, Indonesia, Gabon, Singapore and the United Arab Emirates. She has a M.A. in International Affairs from Sciences Po Paris and a B.A. in Art History from Auburn University. She is currently freelancing in fashion and has worked on such fashion shows as Céline, Hugo Boss and Miu Miu.

NEW YORK, p.12

Laia Garcia was born and raised in Puerto Rico but now lives in Brooklyn. She enjoys collecting magazines, people-watching on the F train, obsessing over crazy shoes and drinking copious amounts of coffee. Her fashion blog can be found at www.geometricsleep.com.

STOCKHOLM, p.178

Andy Carlson has developed advertising creative, commercial motion picture, music video and photo editorial for clients such as Laforet Japan, *Purple* magazine, ACNE and Animal Collective. He lived and worked in Stockholm with the production company Kamisol.com. He recently co-developed the boutique branding, consulting and production firm threenyc.com.

TOKYO, p.144

Dan Bailey has lived in Japan for seven years. He started tokyodandy.com in 2008 to bridge the gap between street fashion and high fashion. His photography ranges from parties for luxury brands such as Gucci, Louis Vuitton and Marc Jacobs to the underground parties thrown by him and his friends. Dan contributes editorials to both street fashion and high-fashion magazines, cementing his cross-over style.

SYDNEY, p.204

Paul Bui is a stylist, creative director and widely published writer. During his four and a half year stint at *Oyster* magazine, Paul led the magazine into an exciting, new creative era. Now freelancing, he is enjoying dividing himself between the worlds of images and words. www.paulbui.tv

LONDON, p.114

Jem Goulding is an award-winning style and music journalist, director and widely published poet. She is a long-standing contributor to publications such as *Wallpaper*, *The Independent*, *Dazed & Confused* and *Rolling Stone*. This year, her most popular published poems are being made into a series of short films. Her second book, *TOUR*, is due out in 2011. www.jemgoulding.com

MILAN, p.84

Ilaria Norsa (top) and **Fabiana Fierotti**, journalists and stylists in their twenties, are respectively senior fashion editor and fashion editor for *PIG*, an independent lifestyle magazine based in Milan. Ilaria is Milanese, and so are her parents and grandparents. She really loves this city and hates people who call it boring; she thinks they are. Fabiana is Sicilian, from Palermo, but has lived in Milan since 2006. She wanted to live in Milan since she was eight years old.

COVER ILLUSTRATION

Jean-Philippe Delhomme is a French artist and illustrator whose work has been published globally in publications such as the *LA Times*, *Departures*, *Travel + Leisure* and *Vogue Nippon*, among many others. In addition, he has written several books of his own including, most recently, *The Cultivated Life* (2009 Rizzoli). His trademark wit, style and satire have gained him the attention of the fashion and design world and he has become among its most celebrated artists, as has his alter ego the "Unknown Hipster", the featured character of his blog (www.unknownhipster.com). He lives and works in New York.

LOS ANGELES, p.234

Maxwell Williams is a writer, curator, actor, and DJ based in Echo Park. He previously held an editorialship at *Tokion* magazine and is currently the Editor of *Flaunt* magazine.

M C A J R S O
B A S O A J B
M A R M J M
M S A C O S A
R J A C B R M
J A B J B R M
S O A J M C S
C J M O R A

NEW YORK

1923 Barneys New York opens in Manhattan

1943 First New York "Press Week" fashion shows held when WWII prevents travel to the Paris Collections

1943 First annual Coty Award presented to Norman Norell

1962 Council of Fashion Designers of America founded to promote U.S. design

1963-1971 Diana Vreeland reigns as the eccentric, visionary editor of *VOGUE*

1968 F.I.T. grad Calvin Klein sells his first collection

1977 Halston holds court as the king of the Studio 54 scene

1981 CFDA Fashion Awards established

1985 Donna Karan introduces her Seven Easy Pieces for effortless dressing

1988 Anna Wintour becomes the editor of *VOGUE*

1993 Marc Jacobs creates his infamous Grunge collection for Perry Ellis

1994 Fashion Week consolidated to the tents at Bryant Park

1998 *Sex and the City* introduces the world to Manolo Blahniks and the Meatpacking District

2002 Opening Ceremony brings emerging international designers to New York

2003 CFDA/*VOGUE* Fashion Fund created to help emerging American designers with grants up to $200,000

2010 CFDA establishes the Fashion Incubator, giving Garment District studio space to 12 up-and-coming names including Prabal Gurung, Grant Krajecki and Waris Ahluwalia

2010 Fashion Week makes its debut at Lincoln Center

THE NEW YORK LOOK

BY LAIA GARCIA

EVERYONE IN NEW YORK CITY WEARS BLACK.

That's the common stereotype, of course. And although a decent percentage of the population subscribes to this notion, New York style is far more complex than just black on black. New York City is, above all, a place where everyone can dress the way they want and individuality is encouraged (required, even). The outrageous becomes a part of the everyday and the mundane often becomes outrageous.

For centuries, independent spirits from all corners of the world have come here seeking freedom of expression, turning the city into a stage for major cultural change. Each neighborhood has its own individual identity, one that shapes (and is shaped by) the sartorial choices of its dwellers. Of course, in a city where everyone is constantly moving forward and looking for the Next Big Thing, nothing can really exist in isolation: every person, culture and idea influences New York style.

Though New York City shares the title of "fashion capital of the world" with Paris, Milan and London, it is possibly the most influential city in terms of what the average person will end up wearing. Nowhere is that more evident than in our own sidewalks. Twice a year, in February and September, the city transforms itself

< (PREVIOUS SPREAD) MARC JACOBS

for Fashion Week. As if our own population of stylists, designers, models, editors, photographers, PR reps and other fashion types wasn't enough, the "fashion people" of everywhere else in the world descend on Manhattan. Everywhere you go you see packs of editors in vertiginous heels, perfectly coiffed hair and big black sunglasses to match their mostly-black outfits. (The percentage of New Yorkers who dress in black increases tenfold when you look at the percentage of New Yorkers who dress in black and work in fashion.) Models, those impossibly tall young girls running around the city from castings to shows, in super skinny jeans and slicked-back hair, carry their portfolios against their chests like Trapper Keepers, making the entire city feel like a never-ending recess. Except

here, the young beauty waiting for the train next to you could also be staring out from the pages of the magazine you're reading to pass the time.

All of these fabulous people are documented by street-style photographers, another reason why New Yorkers will secretly step it up a notch during Fashion Week, whether they work in the business or not. Everyone wants to be photographed. The city's most beloved street-style lensman, Bill Cunningham, has been documenting the exceptionally well dressed

^ (TOP) ANNA SUI'S SOHO FLAGSHIP
(BOTTOM) SOPHOMORE'S SPRING/SUMMER 2010 LOOKBOOK

for the *New York Times* for over 30 years. Spotting his signature blue jacket among the hordes that crowd outside fashion shows is always a delight, even for the most jaded New Yorker (another stereotype, although this one is probably true). While Cunningham documents the scions of upper-class society, *New York* magazine catalogs everyone else with their "Look Book" section. Started in 2004, the classic portrait and Q&A feature is so popular that it was recently compiled into a book. For its release, Barneys—the city's most fashion-forward department store—decorated their windows with photographs from the book. High-fashion and everyday style hanging out next to each other, just like in the real streets of New York.

For much of the 20th century, the New York look was embodied by the society dames of Park Avenue on the Upper East Side, women who traveled the world and dressed accordingly. There was Nan Kempner, who devoted her time to charitable organizations while also amassing an incredible collection of haute couture. Diana Vreeland, the ultimate fashion editor, with stints at both *Harper's Bazaar* and *Vogue*, was famous for her fashion proclamations ("pink is the navy blue of India") and for her impeccable Chanel wardrobe, imported from Paris. These women lived fabulous lives

COSTUME INSTITUTE

Housed in the Metropolitan Museum of Art, the Costume Institute contains one of the world's greatest collections of garments. Its holdings are so delicate that even in the dimly lit space there is no permanent exhibition. Instead the Institute hosts two exhibitions a year. And every May, a who's who of fashion, Hollywood and society meet to fete its spring show at the year's hottest ticket—The Costume Institute Gala.

Thanks to a 2009 partnership with the Brooklyn Museum, the collection includes more than 75,000 items spanning seven centuries—everything from medieval shoes to Alexander McQueen's famed Oyster dress. Under the direction of Harold Koda, recent exhibitions include a Poiret retrospective and a survey of the private collection of society doyenne Iris Apfel.

While its collection dates back centuries, the Institute is very much a living part of fashion; its exhibitions set the tone for fashion and inspire designers.

Even with the garments behind glass, it's the closest you can get to haute couture without spending a fortune. Talk about extreme window-shopping.

Costume Institute
Metropolitan Museum of Art
1000 Fifth Avenue
+1 212 535 7710
WWW.METMUSEUM.ORG

OPENING CEREMONY

Opening Ceremony is a downtown icon with a distinctly global point of view. Opened in 2002 by globe-trotting fashion lovers Humberto Leon and Carol Lim, the shop made its name by importing new designs from fashion-forward destinations including Hong Kong, Germany and Japan. Among the hard-to-find (at least in the U.S.) labels: Swedish powerhouse Acne, Brazil's Alexandre Herchcovitch, and British high-street chain Topshop.

The Opening Ceremony brand now includes a house label, collabs with the likes of style icon Chloë Sevigny and artist Aurel Schmidt, a gallery, and even a showroom to support up-and-coming international designers. Plus three more locations: L.A., Tokyo and New York's Ace Hotel.

35 Howard Street
New York City
+1 212 219 2688
WWW.OPENINGCEREMONY.US

surrounded by beautiful art, clothes and people. Today, Madison Avenue designers such as Oscar de la Renta and Carolina Herrera cater to the uptown crowd with perfectly tailored suits for daytime and luxurious gowns for their many nighttime affairs. That look remains, but by the 1960s, attention had shifted from the uptown chic to the edgy downtown look of Greenwich Village.

Today, it is impossible to pick a specific look that typifies the New Yorker since each neighborhood has its own identity, often shaped by shifts in the art and music scenes. In the 1960s, there wasn't a place more at the center of culture than Andy Warhol's Factory on 47th Street and Third Avenue. The space, famously wallpapered in silver, was a self-contained universe where Warhol worked and partied. Edie Sedgwick was perhaps the most famous member of Warhol's Factory entourage, and one of the first model-slash-actresses. Her eclectic style of black leotards and silver-streaked hair has become synonymous with the era, and has earned

a rightful place next to "sexy cop" in the pantheon of classic Halloween costumes seen in the city every year.

By the late '60s, while the West Coast was seducing the rest of the country with its psychedelic sounds, its barefoot flower-children preaching peace and love, New York City stayed true to its gritty urban roots, never abandoning its love for leather and black. Warhol moved the Factory downtown to Park Avenue South, right smack in the middle of the budding music scene that exploded in the 1970s from the East Village and the Lower East Side. Max's Kansas City, right next to the new Factory location on Park Avenue, and CBGB on the Bowery were the

epicenter of the punk and New Wave explosion. Bands like Television, Blondie, Talking Heads and The Ramones not only changed the musical landscape, but established the classic disaffected youth uniform of torn skinny jeans, washed-til-they-fall-apart T-shirts and beat-up leather jackets that are still worn by the hip downtown kids today. (In the '80s, the Talking Heads became responsible for the popularization of another trend that still lives on, the oversized suit jacket.)

If you journeyed to 54th Street and Eighth Avenue you would have collided head-on with Studio 54 and more glitz and glamour than a high-powered Donna Summer

performance. Here, designers such as Halston found inspiration for the fluid, asymmetric jersey dresses that became the de-rigueur outfit for disco-dancing and the over-the-top attitude that went along with it, a look popularized by movies like *Saturday Night Fever*.

A decade later, Danceteria on 21st Street and Sixth Avenue became the new home of a fresh-from-Detroit Madonna, who, in turn, inspired countless girls to rock black rubber bracelets, mesh shirts and crucifixes. Meanwhile, the new sounds of hip-hop emerged in Queens, Brooklyn and the Bronx, and groups like Run DMC, Grandmaster Flash and Beastie Boys popularized street

^ PATRICIA FIELD'S BOWERY BOUTIQUE AND PUNK LANDMARK TRASH & VAUDEVILLE ON ST. MARK'S PLACE

style and made cultural icons out of Adidas shell-top sneakers.

By the early 21st century, Manhattan was having another fashion moment. With the blockbuster *Sex & the City* TV series and, later, movies like *The Devil Wears Prada,* the rest of the world was introduced to high fashion, designer heels and the general style vibe of Manhattan socialites dressed straight from the pages of *Vogue* (which just happens to have its headquarters in Times Square). The famed TV show's influence is especially evident in the Meatpacking District, where what was once home to actual meat-packing warehouses is now filled with restaurants worthy of Michelin stars and über-hip hotels

REQUIRED READING
Magazines

VOGUE Often regarded as the "fashion Bible", *Vogue* sets the standard for the fashion world at large. **WWW.VOGUE.COM**

ELLE Sleek glossy covering all the latest trends and accessories. **WWW.ELLE.COM**

NEW YORK If you want to know what is happening in New York City right now, pick up this weekly. **WWW.NYMAG.COM**

PAPER Covering designers, actors, artists, club kids, underground legends and the rest of the city's creative contingent for over 25 years.
WWW.PAPERMAG.COM

INTERVIEW Reading *Interview* is like eavesdropping on very important people: actors interview painters, filmmakers interview designers, and the results are always entertaining.
WWW.INTERVIEWMAGAZINE.COM

DOSSIER With just a handful of issues under its belt, *Dossier* has become an essential read for those in the know. Covering topics from fashion to art to literature, *Dossier* also has a Brooklyn concept store, featuring a wide range of items curated by the people who put the magazine together.
WWW.DOSSIERJOURNAL.COM

V The oversized magazine features bold fashion (with a capital F), and talked-about editorials from the people behind limited-edition quarterly *Visionaire.*
WWW.VMAGAZINE.COM

WOMEN'S WEAR DAILY The daily paper with the insider's scoop on everything fashion. **WWW.WWD.COM**

PARSONS

Parsons The New School for Design became a household name for its starring role on *Project Runway*, but it's long been known in the fashion industry as the premier school in the United States for fashion design. While most of its graduates go on to behind-the-scenes gigs at major labels and mass-market brands, Parsons has been churning out top names since Bill Blass enrolled in 1939.

In recent years, a new crop of alumni have been taking their places among fashion's elite, including Jack McCollough and Lazaro Hernandez of Proenza Schouler. The pair cut their teeth as interns for Marc Jacobs (another Parsons alum) and Michael Kors, respectively, and famously had their graduation collection scooped up by Barneys. Other recent grads making waves include Doo-Ri Chung, Jason Wu and Jen Kao plus the duos of Carly Cushnie and Michelle Ochs at Cushnie et Ochs, and Flora Gill and Alexa Adams of Ohne Titel. And then there's wild child *wunderkind* Alexander Wang, who left the school his freshman year to launch his line and never looked back.

For more information visit
WWW.NEWSCHOOL.EDU/PARSONS

preferred by the fashion crowd, like The Standard. Many luxury brands have found a home here as well. Diane von Furstenberg's wildly popular wrap dresses live a few blocks down from Helmut Lang's minimal clothes on Washington Street, and Stella McCartney's animal-friendly designs can be found on 14th Street near Ninth Avenue. And, if we're talking *Sex and the City* fashion, we surely can't leave out the show's fire-tressed costume designer, Patricia Field, who has her own namesake shop further east, on Bowery near Houston, where you can find everything from velvet gloves to sequined cocktail hats.

Around the same time, another music scene was brewing in Williamsburg, Brooklyn. Young adults moved to this borough, one stop away from the resurgent East Village on the L train, in search of cheap rents

^ STUDENTS WORK ON A PROJECT AT PARSONS

and big spaces where they could have art studios and start bands. Bands like The Strokes, Liars and Yeah Yeah Yeahs had a style that was a throwback to the '70s and '80s, but with a twist of modern irony: boys rocked skinny tattered jeans with a shirt, tie, jacket and Converse sneakers as girls played with mismatched vintage. And thus the hipster was born. Since then, the look has changed a bit, going in the opposite direction of its stylistic predecessors. Whereas before it was all about artful tatter and a multi-generational-alterna-youth look, it's not uncommon to see young men and women in slim cut trousers, perfectly fitted button downs and penny loafers—a new twist on the Americana look. Youngsters flock to stores like Rag & Bone on Christopher Street and Bleecker in the West Village, Steven Alan on Franklin Street and Sixth Avenue and France's A.P.C. on Mercer and Prince in Soho for preppy basics that are equal parts classic New England W.A.S.P. and mid-20th-century French New Wave. The unlikely combination results in subverted classics that are all New York at heart.

The early 2000s also saw a shift in the world of high-fashion, with a new crop of American designers with a decidedly New York City attitude. Jack McCollough and Lazaro Hernandez met while students at Parsons, and, after famously selling their entire graduate collection to Barneys, Proenza Schouler was born. Their aesthetic is sophisticated and feminine but always with a slight tomboy twist. The city's current golden boy is Alexander Wang, who in the span of a few years has built a strong following based on the

REQUIRED READING
Blogs

THE MOMENT The coolest new chair, the best café and the must-have shoes can all be found here. It's not New York-centric, but New York-curated. **WWW.TMAGAZINE.BLOGS.NYTIMES.COM**

STYLE.COM Fashion news and photos straight from the runway. **WWW.STYLE.COM**

REFINERY 29 An absolute must-read for the fashion savvy, featuring fashion news, street-style shots, the best sales and an online shop. **WWW.REFINERY29.COM**

MR. NEWTON Eddie Newton searches NYC (and the world) for its most stylish inhabitants. Perfect inspiration for when you're not sure what to wear. **WWW.MRNEWTON.NET**

TERRY'S DIARY Terry Richardson's irreverent photographs have appeared in magazines all over the world. On his blog you're more likely to see pictures of his nightly facials, his favorite flowers or his mom. **WWW.TERRYSDIARY.COM**

FASHIONISTA Fashion news, interviews and Adventures in Copyrights.
WWW.FASHIONISTA.COM

ALTAMIRA NYC Craig Arend documents the city's off-duty models and their fashionable friends. **WWW.ALTAMIRANYC.BLOGSPOT.COM**

STREET PEEPER Street fashion from around the block and around the world. **WWW.STREETPEEPER.COM**

COACD Casting directory Douglas Perrett's insider view of the business. **WWW.COACD.COM**

FEELS LIKE WHITE LIGHTNING Elizabeth Spiridakis writes about fashion, pop culture and life in the Big Apple.
WWW.FEELSLIKEWHITELIGHTNING.COM

"model-off-duty" look that's all about slouchy jeans, paper-thin T-shirts and body-conscious dresses. Other homegrown favorites include Phillip Lim, whose boutique carries his signature minimal, classic clothing for men, women and children (a veritable one-stop shop for the stylish family); Thakoon Panichgul, whose line, Thakoon, is a favorite of First Lady Michelle Obama; and Sophie Buhai and Lisa Mayock's line, Vena Cava, which caters to the hip Brooklyn crowd with their effortless, wildly printed dresses.

In New York, popular scenes eventually die out and the

∧ (TOP) SCREAMING MIMI'S VINTAGE; ZERO MARIA CORNEJO, BLEECKER STREET

hip neighborhoods undoubtedly give way to luxury condos, but the fashion trends they create can seemingly go on forever, jumbled together in new ways for new times.

Because of its history, New York City attracts a variety of people looking to make their dreams come true, whether they want to be musicians, comedians, fashion designers or simply want to give their families a better life than what they had. Everyone is constantly pushing forward, looking to make their lives better (and their rent cheaper) and this same energy propels the city to embrace new things. You spend twenty minutes in the train every morning and afternoon and every time you will get to see a different slice of the population;

it all comes together here. This is where ideas are born, trends are passed on, and though everyone pretends to not notice each other, people-watching is a local sport.

New York will keep growing and remain a breeding ground for artists and intellectuals in every medium. They, in turn, will continue to influence the style and attitudes of the city's residents. Most recently, street-style bloggers have been coming on pilgrimages to the city, distributing our local flavor to all corners of the world. For some New Yorkers, everyday is a photo shoot and you can't possibly step outside without your best look on. After all, you never know when you'll get your fifteen minutes of fame.

^ A PHOTOSHOOT IN THE MEATPACKING DISTRICT; THE GARMENT DISTRICT

SOHO/NOHO/NOLITA

The heart of downtown New York, these three neighborhoods are home to some of the city's best people-watching, plus impossibly hip restaurants and a balance of big-name (Bloomingdale's, Topshop, H&M), brand name (Prada, Apple, A.P.C.) and indie (Oak, Opening Ceremony) shopping.

LOWER EAST SIDE

A younger, scruffier cousin to Soho, the Lower East Side is home to small boutiques and top-notch vintage stores, plus bars, restaurants and galleries, which are starting to branch out into nearby Chinatown.

WEST VILLAGE

This residential neighborhood stays true to its bohemian past with cute restaurants and boutiques on quiet, tree-lined streets, plus the Marc Jacobs retail empire.

EAST VILLAGE

Rock 'n' roll has given way to bank branches and chain stores, but the East Village still retains a bit of edge thanks to its abundance of bars, independent shops and the punk-rock remnants of St. Mark's Place.

MEATPACKING DISTRICT

This pricey neighborhood traded meat-packing plants for the meat market of trendy nightspots. Along with clubs, high-end shopping and showrooms bring stiletto-clad crowds.

CHELSEA

It's all about the art crowd on Manhattan's far West Side. On Thursday night Chelsea's streets are lined with chic crowds hopping from gallery opening to gallery opening. Late night and weekends it turns into clubland.

UPTOWN

The Upper East Side is Manhattan's old-money corridor and Madison Avenue is flanked with designer labels from Calvin Klein to Giorgio Armani, plus the Barneys New York flagship. Meanwhile, just south of Central Park, 57th Street boats big-money boutiques including Chanel and Prada, and the landmark Bergdorf Goodman at Fifth Avenue.

< THE MEATPACKING DISTRICT

THE STANDARD HOTEL
Jet-setters mix with the city's most glamorous at the Boom Boom Room, the exclusive hotspot on the hotel's 18th floor that boasts incredible views of the city—and of the eye candy within.
848 Washington Street
New York City
+1 212 645 4646
WWW.STANDARDHOTELS.COM

THE SMILE
Along with its menu of homey fare—lamb meatballs, roasted chicken and smoked salmon from nearby Russ & Daughters—The Smile offers a well curated selection of books, teas and all-American accessories.
26 Bond Street
New York City
+1 646 329 5836
WWW.THESMILENYC.COM

KENMARE
Kenmare's Paul Sevigny and Nur Khan are kings of a certain brand of upscale New York nightlife. Their scene-y Mediterranean restaurant boasts a basement lounge that hosted a bevy of A-list Fashion Week festivities before the place even opened.
98 Kenmare Street
New York City
+1 212 274 9898

THE ACE HOTEL
The Ace Hotel transformed a previously unfashionable slice of Midtown Manhattan into a bona fide hotspot. Its restaurant, The Breslin Bar & Dining Room, offers up a British-inspired menu from chef April Bloomfield.
20 West 29th Street
New York City
+1 212 679 2222
WWW.ACEHOTEL.COM/NEWYORK

THE JANE HOTEL & BALLROOM
A historic hotel revived into a (relatively) cheap place to stay, with a cushy lounge serving fancy cocktails.
113 Jane Street
New York City
+1 212 924 6700
WWW.THEJANENYC.COM

< THE STANDARD HOTEL

VENA CAVA

Designers Lisa Mayock and Sophie Buhai met at Parsons and launched the Vena Cava label from their living room floor just weeks after graduation. Since then they've become two of the most beloved figures in New York fashion's new wave—both for their enviable personal style and for their intelligent, romantic designs. They recently moved their studio to Soho from the Old American Can Factory near Brooklyn's Gowanus Canal, but the girls still call Brooklyn home—Lisa in Williamsburg and Sophie in Carroll Gardens.

HOW WOULD YOU DESCRIBE THE NEW YORK LOOK?

Lisa Mayock: I'd say that any New York "look" really varies by neighborhood. In my opinion I think the most distinctive, specific to New York look would be the Park Avenue lady. There's definitely a downtown hipster look and a Brooklyn vibe that began in New York but has now spread everywhere. The uptown look is pretty special since you don't really see that vibe anywhere else.

YOU'RE PART OF A NEW WAVE OF YOUNG DESIGNERS THAT'S REDEFINING NEW YORK FASHION. COULD YOU TALK ABOUT THAT?

Sophie Buhai: During the time we gradu-

ated the category of "Young Designer" had not yet been fully developed. There were "Designer" price points and "Contemporary" price points, but nothing in between. During that time there was a huge void in the market for the next generation of designers, designers who would come after Seventh Avenue: The Donnas, Calvins and Ralph Laurens. Since the economy was good, it was the perfect moment for a new emerging generation of designers to mark their place. I think that's why so many of us have survived—it was the right time financially, and there was a need. I'm proud that our generation has created a new category, with clothing that feels designer at a more attainable price point. I don't think we relate to very expensive clothing; we are designing for ourselves and our friends,

and the product is based in reality. It's a newer, more relaxed way to look at fashion.

DOES THE CITY EVER FIND ITS WAY INTO YOUR DESIGNS? HOW SO?

SB: Out of any city in the world New York has the most diversity in terms of the people. Riding the subway and walking the streets, you can't help but notice how people dress. From old ladies to skaters to hip-hop guys there is tons of inspiration everywhere. I think street style and the way people dress around us really influences our eye. There is so much exposure here, we can't help but be affected by it.

WHERE IN THE CITY DO YOU GO TO FIND INSPIRATION?

LM: Quiet places feel the most powerful

here because the level of energy and noise can be really overwhelming at times. I love going to the library. The one on 42nd Street is a gorgeous and serene place to be, even if you're just people-watching, which I find to be the most consistent source of inspiration. The Neue Galerie, and the Frick...I always feel inspired, because of the work that's there, but also the experience of being in such an incredible space.

YOU BOTH COME FROM THE WEST COAST, HOW DOES THAT BACKGROUND INFLUENCE YOUR WORK?

SB: People on the West Coast are less neurotic about trends and having good taste. There is a spontaneity and a comfort that comes with dressing out there. You may come in contact with only a few people each day, so people dress for themselves instead of others. I think there is less pressure out there to be stylish, and more pressure to be comfortable and wear what you feel good in. In New York people wear their clothing like their armor; it's more of urban survival gear. California is softer, more optimistic, and dare I say more "crunchy". I think you see that in our clothes—there's a darkness, and edge, yet it always is balanced with a softer, more psychedelic spontaneity.

TRAVEL SEEMS TO BE A BIG INFLUENCE IN YOUR WORK, WHAT ARE SOME OF YOUR

FAVORITE PLACES?

LM: Jaipur and Udaipur in India for their street food and color sensibility. It's amazing and completely different from how we view colors in the United States. Kinugawa, Japan, for their wild monkeys and hot springs. Paris for walking around with headphones on—they also get bonus points for having the best subway map. And Buenos Aires for antiques and good parties.

LOOKING BACK AT YOUR PAST COLLECTIONS, WHAT ARE SOME OF YOUR FAVORITE MOMENTS?

LM: I loved our Egyptomania collection and our Crystalarium collection. We got to learn about hieroglyphics, the '70s Occult movement, and gems and minerals. This job is great when you get to research weird stuff at the library all day.

WHAT ADVICE WOULD YOU GIVE FOR SOMEONE TRYING TO MAKE IT IN THE WORLD OF NEW YORK FASHION?

SB: Don't ever become "fabulous." Be nice to people, and work with your friends rather than corporate people. Design things that are personal.

For more on Vena Cava visit **WWW.VENACAVANYC.COM**. To read about their inspirations—including travel, music and old VHS tapes—visit their blog at **WWW.VIVAVENACAVA.BLOGSPOT.COM.**

SNAP STAR
EDDIE NEWTON

As street photographers take over the web, Eddie Newton's eye for style has placed him at the top of the pack. Along the way, his photos of cool young things have appeared in top magazines around the world, from the U.S. (teenVOGUE, Seventeen, New York, Lucky) to Australia, from Italy to Japan.

WHAT DOES IT TAKE FOR SOMEONE TO CATCH YOUR EYE?

It's difficult to describe what it is that catches my eye, but it's very clear when I'm out on the street shooting—there is rarely any hesitation or doubt. I guess the best way of phrasing it would be "I know it when I see it." Often I will be intrigued only by certain elements—or a single element—of a person's outfit. It's rare that their entire head-to-toe look will catch my eye. I often zero-in on accessories and seemingly minor parts of a person's outfit: hats, belts, shoes, eyeglasses, tights or hosiery. These are the things that pull an outfit together and give it direction and a signature. Also—let's not kid ourselves—physical attractiveness often looms large in the street fashion world. A great outfit is wonderful, but a gorgeous girl with a great outfit? Well, then you really have something special.

HAVE YOU PICKED UP ANY TIPS PHOTOGRAPHING SO MANY STYLISH PEOPLE?

The number one tip that I've picked up would be to "keep it simple." With so much fashion information and so many fashion images at our fingertips these days, one sometimes needs to remind oneself that less is more when it comes to

personal style. This is especially true for a man; women can experiment more with things like color, whimsical elements, vintage pieces and clashing prints.

HOW WOULD YOU DESCRIBE THE NEW YORK LOOK?

The New York look is geek chic with a rock 'n' roll edge and an eye on new trends in other fashion capitals, all generally done in a low-key and tasteful manner that makes a statement without shouting. The geek chic thing is particularly hot right now, not only are there lots of nerd glasses and plaid shirts and boat shoes on the street, but some of the hottest designers and stores are featuring an almost orthopedic aesthetic. New York, too, is the home of rock 'n' roll style. And by "rock 'n' roll style" I really mean "pop music style," which can incorporate everything from authentic old-school '80s hip-hop influences to the outfit that Lady Gaga was wearing around

town just last night. Also, New Yorkers really stay up-to-date with emerging trends in other fashion capitals. Trends from Paris, Stockholm, Sydney, London and Tokyo arrive here almost immediately; making sure New York stays well ahead of other U.S. cities in terms of style.

HOW DO YOU DEFINE NEW YORK CITY STYLE?

New York City style to me means Manhattan style, and Manhattan style means downtown style. However, there are uniquely stylish people all across the city. I'm making an effort these days to shoot street fashion in some of the city's more far-flung neighborhoods.

DO YOU HAVE GO-TO NEIGHBORHOODS TO PHOTOGRAPH?

Soho on a weekday late morning or early afternoon is fantastic for street style, possibly the best neighborhood in the world for this.

I've shot street fashion in trendy neighborhoods from Harajuku to Södermalm, and there's nowhere that's better. You have members of almost every stylish tribe all within one compact area: fashion editors, off-duty models, stylish celebs, people from the art world, fashion designers, fashionable tourists from around the world, and—considering that it's quite a posh neighborhood—a surprisingly large number of indie/hipster kids who might be shopping at Topshop, checking out a show at an edgy Soho gallery like Team, or maybe just passing through on their way to lunch at La Esquina or Cafe Gitane in Nolita.

Not only do you have a great variety of stylish people to shoot, but the neighborhood itself is very photogenic. The cobblestone streets and cast-iron buildings make great backdrops for street fashion photography.

On the weekends, Soho feels completely different and is a definite no-go area for me. It's overrun with hordes of mainstream shoppers and the stylish tribes all disappear as if on cue. Other neighborhoods that I often shoot in are Nolita, the Lower East Side, the West Village and Meatpacking District, and the west Chelsea gallery district. On weekends, when most areas of Manhattan become more mainstream and crowded, I often shoot stylish indie kids around Bedford Avenue in Williamsburg, Brooklyn.

WHAT ESSENTIAL ELEMENTS SHOULD ALL NEW YORKERS HAVE IN THEIR WARDROBES?
Geek glasses: The simplest way to convey a certain downtown, arty intellectualism.

A stylish but functional bag: As the only true "walking city" in the U.S., most New Yorkers do not have the luxury of using their car as a mobile storage unit while out doing their daily business or errands. Therefore, guys and girls alike need a cool bag of some sort for carrying around all of their stuff.

Cool-but-comfortable shoes: It's the walking thing again. We do a lot of it, but we still need to look good. I like Topshop wedges for girls and something from the boat shoe family from Opening Ceremony for guys.

A great pair of jeans: Jeans are the ultimate day-to-night staple. For guys, A.P.C. makes the best jeans; for girls I like J Brand.

A cool vintage bike: Forget everything I've said about NYC being a walking city, lately the downtown fashion crowd are all cruising around on vintage bicycles from the '60s and '70s. Check out the selection at trendy Landmark Vintage Bicycles in the East Village.

YOU TRAVEL ALL OVER THE WORLD. WHEN IT COMES TO STYLE HOW DOES NEW YORK STACK UP AGAINST OTHER CITIES?

Having shot street fashion everywhere from Sydney to Tokyo, Copenhagen to Capri, I can say honestly that New York is the most stylish city in the world. Paris during Fashion Week is more stylish than New York during Fashion Week, but during most of the year—that is, on just a regular Tuesday—there are far more stylish people walking around New York than you will find in Paris on an equivalent day. Other cities like London and Stockholm are extremely stylish but the fashionable folks tend to be confined to a select few neighborhoods or tend to wear a handful of accepted "looks" of the season. Other cities excel in certain areas of style, but the depth and breadth of New York style is unmatched.

To see Mr. Newton's take on the latest looks around the globe visit **WWW.MRNEWTON.NET**

MR. NEWTON'S NEW YORK

In New York? Check out some of Mr. Newton's favorite things to do:

1. Pull a stool up to the counter at La Esquina for tacos, grilled corn, and homemade *agua de sandia*.

2. In the summer, go to the free Pool Parties on the waterfront in Williamsburg. (There's no pool, just free concerts with hot indie bands and DJs.) It's a great spot for checking out the coolest and cutest indie kids.

3. Visit Coney Island—one of the last places where you can feel the energy and attitude of raw, unrefurbished 1970s New York.

4. Find a deal on Saturdays and Sundays at the Brooklyn Flea, featuring hundreds of vendors in two locations.

5. Take the LIRR out to Montauk and swim at fashionably rugged Ditch Plains beach and stay a night or two at the awesomely unspoiled 1950s-era East Deck Motel.

BIRD
BROOKLYN

Jennifer Mankins is the owner of Bird, a Brooklyn boutique that's a favorite with fashionistas from all five boroughs. Each shop offers a selection of designs from international and local labels including Apiece Apart, Bodkin and Loeffler Randall, as well as artsy accessories and home goods. Mankins travels the globe in search of good design, but she's proud to call Brooklyn home.

HOW WOULD YOU DESCRIBE BIRD?

I like to think of Bird as accessible, approachable fashion. It is my mission to make every store as warm and friendly as possible and to provide excellent customer service and product knowledge, so no matter if you are shopping for a $30 El Paso tote bag or a $1500 Proenza Schouler PS1 bag, you will have an excellent, fun shopping experience.

WHO IS YOUR CUSTOMER?

My customers are very knowledgeable about fashion and style and always looking for exciting new designers. They want beautiful, independent designs that have history and integrity.

HOW DO YOU SPOT NEW TALENT?

I am lucky to live and work in Brooklyn, one of the most prolific and creative cities in the world. I am inundated daily with calls and e-mails from new designers looking to show me their collections. I try to give everyone a look, because you never know when you might stumble upon the next big thing. I also travel constantly and always have my eyes peeled for new talent wherever I happen to find myself.

IS THERE A "BROOKLYN LOOK"?

Brooklyn is very diverse and it would be hard to say it has one definitive "look", but I would say the best word to describe it would be independent. My customers are smart and confident and they want their clothes to reflect that. They look for special, interesting designs. They know about the latest trends and designers, but they are always going to put their own spin on it.

YOU HAVE SHOPS ALL OVER BROOKLYN. HOW ARE THESE NEIGHBORHOODS DIFFERENT?

I tailor all of the shops to each specific neighborhood, so they each have their own personality. Williamsburg is the most fashion-forward with a very cutting-edge clientele. We also have our largest men's shop at that location so we have tons of super-stylish men coming through the shop everyday. Park Slope, on the other hand, has a mature, classic vibe happening, while Cobble Hill falls somewhere in the middle.

WHAT BROOKLYN DESIGNERS ARE YOU MOST EXCITED ABOUT RIGHT NOW?

Bodkin by Eviana Hartman reflects all of the things I find most exciting and inspiring. Every piece is thoughtful and beautiful, but very functional and cool and it is all produced with the highest ethical standards here in NYC from completely sustainable fabrics. It is modern and smart yet remains very easy to wear and fits a lot of different ages and body types.

WHY IS BROOKLYN AN EXCITING PLACE TO RUN A BUSINESS?

I said it before, but will say it again, Brooklyn is the best! Just last night I was remarking that I was so lucky to live here because it really has the highest concentra-

tion of smart, cool, creative people of any city, anywhere. The food scene, the music scene, the fashion and design scene, I can't think of anywhere more dynamic or inspiring, or anywhere I'd rather live and work.

BIRD COBBLE HILL
220 Smith Street
Brooklyn, New York
+1 718 797 3774

BIRD PARK SLOPE
316 Fifth Avenue
Brooklyn, New York
+1 718 768 4940

BIRD WILLIAMSBURG
203 Grand Street
Brooklyn, New York
+1 718 388 1655

For more on Bird visit **WWW.SHOPBIRD.COM**

THE ICONS

CALVIN KLEIN

What started as a line of coats has become an international empire. The so-called Master of Minimalism ruled the '90s with superb tailoring and a monochromatic palette. While the clothes were all about subtlety, his iconic denim ads defined the in-your-face sexuality of the decade. Since Klein left the company, designers Francisco Costa (womenswear) and Italo Zucchelli (menswear) have maintained the classic Calvin aesthetic while pushing the brand into the 21st century.

654 Madison Avenue
New York City
+1 212 292 9000
WWW.CALVINKLEININC.COM

DONNA KARAN

Since 1984, the "Queen of Seventh Avenue" has designed wardrobe essentials for working women, including a collection of seven mix-and-match jersey basics. Her range has expanded beyond her famous bodysuits, but whether it's a suit or a glamorous gown, there is always a sense of empowerment through practicality in Karan's clothes. She launched DKNY, the first successful designer diffusion line in 1989, and was awarded the CFDA's Lifetime Achievement Award in 2004.

819 Madison Avenue
New York City
+1 212 861 1001
WWW.DONNAKARAN.COM

CALVIN KLEIN

DONNA KARAN

MARC JACOBS

Marc Jacobs has been making a stamp on the New York fashionscape for over 20 years. His 1993 Grunge collection for Perry Ellis famously got him fired from the label, allowing him to focus on his own line. Since then, Jacobs has reinvented American sportswear with old-world class and a touch of New York humor. He's added a secondary line, Marc by Marc Jacobs, fragrances, children's clothes and even a bookstore to his portfolio, perfectly defining the lifestyle brand.

163 Mercer Street
New York City
+1 212 343 1490
WWW.MARCJACOBS.COM

RALPH LAUREN

Ralph Lauren has been in the fashion business since he was in high school, when he still went by the last name Lifshitz and sold ties to his schoolmates. He made his foray into the proper world of fashion in the 1970s, with a collection of women's suits cut in masculine silhouettes. A few years later he released his classic short-sleeve shirt with the monogrammed Polo player on the chest. It became an instant classic and a symbol of the all-American look, establishing Lauren as an American icon.

867 Madison Avenue
New York City
+1 212 606 2100
WWW.RALPHLAUREN.COM

MARC JACOBS

RALPH LAUREN

THE ESTABLISHMENT

ANNA SUI

Known for her wonderful prints and rocker-chick aesthetic, Anna Sui has been the queen of the downtown cool since the inception of her label in the early '90s. Her hip Soho store also features her range of makeup, accessories as well as selections from her vintage collection of dresses and rock posters.

WWW.ANNASUI.COM

BETSEY JOHNSON

Betsey Johnson's love for all things girly and fun has made her a mainstay of the New York fashion scene for over 30 years. Her early designs have recently been reissued proving that her feminine charm is, in its own way, timeless.

WWW.BETSEYJOHNSON.COM

CAROLINA HERRERA

Carolina Herrera may be from Venezuela, but her luxurious clothes have come to define a certain kind of Upper East Side chic. Bold colors in sumptuous fabrics are the norm for this former outfitter of Jackie Kennedy.

WWW.CAROLINAHERRERA.COM

DIANE VON FURSTENBERG

Her jersey wrap dresses created a sensation in the '70s and since then Diane von Furstenberg has created a bona fide fashion empire. Her clothes are bold, classic and an unabashed celebration of being a woman.

WWW.DVF.COM

MICHAEL KORS

No one makes more proudly American clothes than Michael Kors. Whether it's reworking basics in a new way or creating glamorous red-carpet gowns, his confident creations are unparalleled.

WWW.MICHAELKORS.COM

NARCISO RODRIGUEZ

Narciso Rodriguez designs thoroughly modern body-conscious dresses that are striking and flattering. He is a favorite of first lady Michelle Obama, who wore one

ANNA
SUI

DIANE
VON FURSTENBERG

MICHAEL
KORS

of his dresses on the night Barack Obama was elected president.
WWW.NARCISORODRIGUEZ.COM

OSCAR DE LA RENTA
Dominican-born designer Oscar de la Renta has been at the center of New York fashion for more than 40 years. His love of luxury and the well-dressed woman is reflected in his use of bold colors and ruffles and it's definitely the reason why celebrities flock to him for their red carpet gowns.
WWW.OSCARDELARENTA.COM

VERA WANG
Vera Wang made her name as the go-to-gal for wedding dresses, but ever since she expanded her range to include ready-to-wear, women have been flocking to her for easy dresses in fashion-forward cuts and stand-out jewelry.
WWW.VERAWANG.COM

STORES

ANNA SUI
113 Greene Street
New York City
+1 212 941 8406

BETSEY JOHNSON
138 Wooster Street
New York City
+1 212 995 5048

CAROLINA HERRERA
954 Madison Avenue
New York City
+1 212 249 6552

DIANE VON FURSTENBERG
874 Washington Street
New York City
+1 646 486 4800

MICHAEL KORS
974 Madison Avenue
New York City
+1 212 452 4685

OSCAR DE LA RENTA
772 Madison Avenue
New York City
+1 212 288 5810

VERA WANG
158 Mercer Street
New York City
+1 212 382 2184

NARCISO RODRIGUEZ

OSCAR DE LA RENTA

VERA WANG

THE NEW WAVE

3.1 PHILLIP LIM

Since launching his line in 2005, Phillip Lim has become a finalist for the CFDA Fashion Awards, collaborated with Gap and launched a line of "green" clothes for Barneys. His clothes are easy to wear, often with extraordinary details like the oversized T-shirt dress with fabric flowers that first brought him to the limelight.

115 Mercer Street
New York City
+1 212 334 1160

WWW.31PHILLIPLIM.COM

ALEXANDER WANG

Alexander Wang has built a fashion empire from the model-off-duty uniform: slouchy T-shirts, menswear-inspired pieces and supremely sexy dresses. Still in his twenties, he has already established himself as a fashion force, and with the recent introduction of bags and shoes, it's clear that he has what it takes for the long haul. **WWW.ALEXANDERWANG.COM**

CUSHNIE ET OCHS

Carly Cushnie and Michelle Ochs have established a label that is young and sophisticated with body-conscious, sharply tailored dresses that stand out in any setting. **WWW.CUSHNIEETOCHS.COM**

DOO.RI

Since the beginning of her career, Doo-Ri Chung's masterfully draped jersey dresses have been winning her awards in the industry, and it's easy to see why. Her elegant creations are suited for almost any body type and can easily go from day to night.

WWW.DOORI-NYC.COM

JASON WU

Jason Wu is one of the younger designers of the New York fashion scene, but his aesthetic is decidedly mature, drawing inspiration from fashion masters like Jacques Fath. **WWW.JASONWUSTUDIO.COM**

3.1
PHILLIP LIM

ALEXANDER
WANG

JASON
WU

OHNE TITEL

The name may be German, but the label founded by Flora Gill and Alexa Adams is New York at heart. The duo's innovative use of textures and their razor-pin silhouettes have made the label the place to go for women who want to dress in clothes from the future, now. **WWW.OHNETITEL.COM**

PHILIP CRANGI

Philip Crangi's jewelry is steeped in traditional materials and processes, but aesthetically it's all about charming modern classics. Recently he established a lower price line, Giles & Brother.
9 Ninth Avenue,
New York City
+1 212 929 0858
WWW.PHILIPCRANGI.COM

PROENZA SCHOULER

Jack McCollough and Lazaro Hernandez met while students at Parsons, and their senior collection was bought by famed department store Barneys. They've been on a stellar trajectory since then, injecting their brand of downtown cool to clothes, shoes and accessories that manage to be both effortlessly hip and timeless. **WWW.PROENZASCHOULER.COM**

THAKOON

After clocking in some time working for *Harper's Bazaar*, Thakoon Panichgul decided he wanted to be on the other side of the pages, and launched his line to critical acclaim. His clothes feature classic cuts in bright prints. **WWW.THAKOON.COM**

VENA CAVA

Lisa Mayock and Sophie Buhai hail from California, but in the 10 years that they've lived in the city, they have definitely adopted certain New York sensibilities into their wildly successful line of quirky-chic dresses that often have a mystical inspiration behind them. **WWW.VENACAVANYC.COM**

OHNE TITEL

THAKOON

VENA CAVA

THE UNDERGROUND

BLACK SHEEP & PRODIGAL SONS

Derrick Cruz creates jewelry influenced by the occult, finding beauty in unlikely places like honey combs and old piano keys.

WWW.BLACKSHEEPANDPRODIGALSONS.COM

JEN KAO

Over several seasons Jen Kao has perfected a sleek downtown sex appeal.

WWW.JENKAO.COM

KATIE GALLAGHER

This Rhode Island School of Design grad burst onto the scene with a strong point of view that is equal parts goth and romantic.

WWW.KATIEGALLAGHER.COM

MARY MEYER

Mary Meyer's easy-going Brooklyn-by-way-of-California attitude is reflected in her trademark "biggie" silhouette, an oversized one-size-fits-all T-shirt, often decorated with minimalist geometric shapes.

WWW.MARYMEYERCLOTHING.COM

ORGANIC

John Patrick's simple, sophisticated design's aren't just wearable, they're also eco-friendly.

WWW.JOHNPATRICKORGANIC.COM

PAMELA LOVE

Jewelry designer Pamela Love is instantly recognizable on the streets of Manhattan with her long, dark tresses and the aura of mystery that surrounds her. Her in-demand jewelry culls inspiration from sources such as birds and the Mexican Day of the Dead festivities.

WWW.PAMELALOVENYC.COM

PATRIK ERVELL

Patrik Ervell was an editor at *V* magazine before launching his label in 2005 and earning a CFDA/*Vogue* Fashion Fund nomination. His clothes reflect a modern masculinity and a hint of intellectualism, making them a favorite of artsy guys.

WWW.PATRIKERVELL.COM

JEN KAO

KATIE GALLAGHER

PAMELA LOVE

PRABAL GURUNG

Prabal Gurung has become one to watch, especially since First Lady Michelle Obama started sporting his designs. Trained by Cynthia Rowley and Bill Blass, he makes beautiful clothes with a dose of luxury. **WWW.PRABALGURUNG.COM**

SLOW & STEADY WINS THE RACE

Mary Ping's designs are a send-up to the fashion biz, with conceptual projects that rethink classic garments, such as the plain white T-shirt or a black-leather version of the plastic bag. **SLOWANDSTEADYWINSTHERACE.COM**

SOPHOMORE

Chrissie Miller's Sophomore line is all about the quintessential Lower East Side wardrobe: the perfect T-shirt. With the addition of designer Madeleine von Froomer, the label has expanded to include a range of super-cool jackets and dresses. **WWW.SOPHOMORENYC.COM**

THREEASFOUR

threeASFOUR is one of the few survivors of a late-'90s downtown boom that was as much about performance and art as it was about fashion. The label embodies the avant-garde while remaining wearable. **WWW.THREEASFOUR.COM**

TIM HAMILTON

Tim Hamilton made his name in menswear before launching a line of minimal womenswear in 2009. **WWW.TIMHAMILTON.COM**

ZERO + MARIA CORNEJO

Maria Cornejo opened the store Zero in 1998. Now known for her ultra-modern clothes that exude quiet sophistication, she surely will not remain part of the underground much longer.

33 Bleecker Street
New York City
+1 212 925 3849

WWW.ZEROMARIACORNEJO.COM

SOPHOMORE

TIM HAMILTON

ZERO + MARIA CORNEJO

PARIS

1860–1960 The Belle Époque establishes Paris as the world's leading fashion capital

1868 Chambre Syndicale de la Haute Couture established as a
trade union for fashion industry

1903 Paul Poiret establishes his label, creating relaxed
clothing and freeing women from the corset

1909 Gabrielle Bonheur "Coco" Chanel establishes her eponymous
line with modern clothing for the 20th century woman

1945 Chambre de commerce et d'industrie de Paris
establishes the criteria for haute couture

1947 Christian Dior introduces the "New Look": full skirt, full bust and a skinny waist

1966 Yves Saint Laurent launches the first successful ready-to-wear
line and the iconic Le Smoking suit

1985 Karl Lagerfeld appointed creative director of Chanel

1987 A merger creates the massive Louis Vuitton Moët Hennessy luxury empire

1992 *Purple* magazine launched by Elein Fleiss and Olivier Zahm

1997 Colette opens, bringing the curated lifestyle boutique concept to rue Saint-Honoré

2001 Carine Roitfeld becomes editor of *Vogue Paris*, gives
the magazine an edgier, more Parisian style

2009 Christian Lacroix files for bankruptcy

2010 Phoebe Philo returns to fashion; wows critics with her debut for Céline

FRENCH ACCENT

BY LAUREN DRABLIER

As the great Coco Chanel put it, "Fashion is not something that exists in dresses only. Fashion is in the sky, in the street, fashion has to do with ideas, the way we live, what is happening." In Paris, beauty surrounds us. It is the architecture, the art, the streets, the parks, the food. Everything astonishes, takes our breath away and leads us to wonder: How can a place be so beautiful, so elegant? The wonder and magnificence are so overwhelming that it's hard to pinpoint the single feature that makes the city so special.

One thing is certain: In Paris, style is a way of life.

< (PREVIOUS SPREAD) MARAIS BISTRO LE PROGRÈS

The city's signature sense of style is reflected throughout Paris—attention to the finest detail on every building; beautiful presentations in every shop window; modesty, even in all things grand; appreciation and respect for the finer things in life such as wine, fresh food, a bright blue sky and a two-hour lunch break. Life here is not about flash, not about standing out or wearing what is most expensive. It is about understated elegance, about that one item that makes an outfit, and not where you found it. It is attention to detail and presentation; not how many accessories you can add to your outfit. (Madame Chanel always advised French women to "take one item off before leaving the house.") Most of all, Parisian style is about self-discovery, just like the process of discovering the city that surrounds the style.

One thing that stands out in Paris is just how confident and comfortable everyone looks. Parisians are the masters of dressing in what flatters them the most, not what they think *should* look flattering. Rarely do you see a woman struggling to walk in heels or man wearing a poorly fitted jacket. Here the concept of trying to wear something because you think it looks good does not exist. Parisian fashion embodies elegance

^ (CLOCKWISE FROM LEFT)THE EIFFEL TOWER AND THE SEINE; DEPARTMENT STORE LE BON MARCHÉ; GIVENCHY AT LE BON MARCHÉ

and comfort. Whether it is a man's sweater or a little black dress paired with six-inch heels, each Parisian dresses to make herself *feel good*.

Like any city, Paris is a sum of its parts, each home to certain styles that make up an eclectic whole. Nothing here is out of the ordinary except trying to be flashy. Parisians respect a well-put-together outfit, but deem it unacceptable to purposefully try to be brazen. The colors are neutral, yet the outfits are vibrant. Take, for example, Céline's Spring/Summer 2010 collection: comfort, elegance and simplicity. Cinched trench coats, powerful yet feminine trousers and demure leather dresses—this is Paris.

It's a reflection of respect for their city and for themselves. Parisians will always make an effort when

they choose their outfits. You will never see a Parisian leaving the house on a Sunday morning wearing a pair of sweatpants. Never.

The late Yves Saint Laurent said it best: "Dressing is a way of life." And the best way to understand the different styles in this city is to immerse yourself in that life: walk around. Shop at the markets (buy fresh on Saturday and Sunday). Watch the people. Stroll through the upscale, dauntingly expensive areas of Avenue Montaigne and the Champs-Elysées; the eternally elegant Saint-Germain-des-Prés; the trendy Rue du Faubourg Saint-Honoré and Le Marais (always bustling with the who's-who of the Paris fashion scene). Visit the young bobo (bourgeois-bohemian) areas of Oberkampf, Abbesses and Pigalle,

home to eclectic boutiques and vintage stores. Shop at the *puces* of Saint-Ouen, where, beyond urban trends, the inner depths of the markets are filled with pure class. On Sunday afternoons, the *puces* are full of stylists, decorators, designers and hunters of everything unique.

For more insight into the classic Parisian look (which never goes out of style) the destination is Saint-Germain-des-Prés. Get a table outside at the Café de Flore and observe the people passing by. Everything that is wonderful about this city will pass before your very eyes: the fur-clad 75-year-old women walking (or carrying) their mini-dogs with Hermès bags in tote; the young bobo Parisians; boys with their skinny jeans, pointy dress shoes, cardigans and well-tailored jackets; bobo girls

with their tights, heels, layers, scarves and jackets. They all exhibit a certain balance of totally deconstructed—and totally put back together again—style. Sort of like they just happened to fall into that fabulous outfit this morning. Effortless elegance at its very best.

Amid the many grand Parisian boutiques, art galleries and antique dealers of Saint-Germain do not miss the rue des Saints Pères. Full of up-scale boutiques and designer stores, it boasts everything from elegant flower stores (like Mr. Pitou, who caters to the stars), to Prada, Maje and Paul & Joe. Rue du Four and rue de Buci are two more streets that should not be missed. In the area is also Ladurée, producer of the great-est macarons in Paris and a perfect spot for an afternoon tea. On the rue du Bac, which must not be forgot-

ten, the young and old head into
Le Bon Marché, a Parisian department store at its very best. Open the
doors and a whole world opens up, a
world of fashion, life, art, people, the
rich, where everything is beautiful,
smells nice and is soft to the touch.

The window displays are always
a remarkable adventure for
the onlooker. Venture upstairs
and discover fashion exhibits
that change every few months;
anything from a video installation
of photographer Guy Bourdin's

∧ LE BON MARCHÉ

work, to a Lanvin capsule collection, to an homage to the fashion of Los Angeles. Anything goes, but it's always fashion-oriented and always insightful.

Walking from Palais Royale to Place Vendôme via Saint-Honoré on a Saturday afternoon is the greatest pleasure for any-one who loves fashion. Not only are the shops some of the most prominent and trend-setting in Paris, so are the people. The area is always full of the fashion industry's finest. You are sure to bump into a designer or some other big name on this street. Everyone here is dressed to perfection, all sporting clothes seem-ingly designed specially for them. (This is a trait of a true Parisian: knowing how to put together that perfect outfit and taking the time to find something that fits perfectly.) At 213 rue Saint-Honoré, Colette is home to everything that is cool, from books, to clothes, to food, art and music—it is all there and so is the crowd. One should also check out the Marché

REQUIRED READING
Blogs

PURPLE DIARY
A behind-the-scenes (and often X-rated) look into the jet set life of *Purple* magazine's Olivier Zahm and his fabulous friends.
WWW.PURPLE-DIARY.COM

GARANCE DORÉ
Illustrator and photographer Garance Doré wins fans for her sophisticated feminine style and charmingly personal posts.
WWW.GARANCEDORE.FR/EN

A SHADED VIEW ON FASHION
Paris-based fashion journalist and curator Diane Pernet reports from beneath the shade of her signature mantilla.
WWW.ASHADEDVIEWONFASHION.COM

JAK & JIL
Tommy Ton may have gotten his start in Toronto, but nobody captures Paris Fashion Week quite like this photographer.
WWW.JAKANDJIL.COM

THE CHERRY BLOSSOM GIRL
Blogger and budding designer Alix Bancourt is known for sweet style in her clothing and décor: think lots of floral prints, romantic white blouses and pastels.
WWW.THECHERRYBLOSSOMGIRL.COM

THE CHIC MUSE
Stylist Denni Elias was born in Mexico and lives in Paris. Her signature look is classic Parisian chic: red lips and sky-high heels.
WWW.THECHICMUSE.BLOGSPOT.COM

^AN EXHIBIT ON CONTEMPORARY DESIGN AT LE BON MARCHÉ

REQUIRED READING
MAGAZINES

VOGUE PARIS
The most avant-garde member of the *Vogue* family is just like its editor Carine Roitfeld—tousled, sexy, totally Parisian and with a touch of black leather.

WWW.VOGUE.FR

PURPLE
A cutting-edge magazine with oodles of sex appeal, *Purple* covers the best in art and fashion, featuring collaborations with leaders from both scenes.

WWW.PURPLE.FR

NUMÉRO
Sexy, grown up and avant-garde monthly magazine *Numéro* is a leader in the fashion world.

WWW.NUMERO-MAGAZINE.COM

L'OFFICIEL
Since 1926 *L'Officiel* has brought high-end fashion to its ritzy and sophisticated clientele.

WWW.JALOUGALLERY.COM

JALOUSE
The younger, trendier little sister of *L'Officiel*, *Jalouse* features daring editorials with funky styling.

WWW.JALOUSE.FR

SELF SERVICE
Hi-end fashion biannual *Self Service* features some of the most boundary-pushing fashion and design in the biz, all wrapped up in a hardcover.

WWW.SELFSERVICEMAGAZINE.COM

Saint-Honoré, Dalia and Rose, Lanvin and Stéphane Verdino while on this stroll.

Another gem in Paris is le Marais. The Marais, or "the marsh", is part of the old Paris and located right in the heart of the city. In this area of the Rive Droit, the streets are much narrower and the buildings older and smaller than in the rest of the city, It is a great place to walk around on a Sunday afternoon. Most of the stores are open on Sunday and it's generally bustling with locals, tourists and those out to have a relaxing evening browsing the shops or savoring a glass of wine with friends in one of the neighborhood's cafés. In the Marais you can find stores such as COS (Collection of Style), H&M's upscale offshoot. There are also a number of vintage stores in the area. Rue Ste-Croix-de-la Bretonnerie is home to a number of crowed, over-stuffed shops with some great finds ... if you can handle the hunt! Another vintage store worth

^ SUNDAY SHOPPING AT A PARISIAN FLEA MARKET

checking out is Kiliwatch. Nearby boutiques such as Zadig & Voltaire and Sandro carry all the basics for a truly Parisian outfit, from T-shirts and oversized sweatshirts to black sequin vests. When in the area, one should also go to the Marché des Enfants Rouge and Rose Bakery for brunch.

The term "bobo" was coined by *New York Times* columnist David Brooks in 2000 to describe the new upper class. In Paris, it defines a generation that is rich but embraces bohemian style. In practice, it describes those who reflect the notion that life is a balance of effort and effortlessness—that to be beautiful means looking effortless yet put-together at the same time.

That "bobo-chic" look is arguably the quintessential look of young

Paris. It can be found in areas such as Oberkampf and Canal Saint-Martin, or further north, in Abbesses. Rue des Abbesses and rue Lepic (where a large part of the film *Amélie* was shot) are fabulous areas to shop or just spend the afternoon walking around. Rue des Abbesses runs along the base of Montmartre (a 425-foot hill) which was once home to many of the most famous artists including Pablo Picasso, Henri de Toulouse-Lautrec and Edgar Degas. Heading down around the raunchy Pigalle district you'll find Andrea Crews, a young artist collective that transforms vintage and dead-stock items into one-of-a-kind pieces.

After a day of shopping, Hôtel Amour is a great destination for a Sunday brunch if you want to see more stylish Parisians.

Younger designers in Paris are not afraid of pushing the limits that have been set for so long. There is much more color and mixture of textures and prints, which reflects the variety of cultures present in the city.

Alexis Mabille is pushing the limits of traditional Parisian style and taking a more artistic approach with colors and prints. Valentine Gauthier creates striking collections by mixing colors, textures and fabrics all while keeping it simple. At Heimstone, a boutique which opened in 2007, the designers use basic fabrics and add little, unexpected details crafted out of metal and leather to add a bit of edge to otherwise girly looks.

Even big-name designers are introducing more prints and color into their collections. (See the Spring/Summer 2010 collection of Belgian designer Dries Van Noten, which featured an explosion of colorful fabrics including Indian embroideries and handwoven Uzbek ikat at Paris Fashion Week.) The newer generations offer a refreshing and eclectic representation of the world around them all the while respecting that certain Parisian sophistication.

As Ernest Hemingway declared, "If you are lucky enough to have lived in Paris as a young man, then wherever you go for the rest of your life it stays with you, for Paris is a moveable feast." A taste will stay with you, lingering in every part of your existence.

Paris is about the balance between the young and the old, between innovation and the legacy of iconic maisons like Christian Dior, Chanel, Yves Saint Laurent, Sonia Rykiel,

HAUTE COUTURE

While the term haute couture gets thrown around a lot, its meaning is actually quite specific—and protected by the Chambre Syndicale de la Haute Couture.

To qualify, labels must show twice yearly with no fewer than 35 looks, create custom clothing made-to-order and have an atelier employing at least 15 people.

These one-of-a-kind creations feature luxurious fabrics, rich embroidery and embellishment created by hand, by "petit mains," the specialized craftswomen behind the big-name design houses, often costing into the tens of thousands of dollars per garment—and up.

Current members of this elite club include Chanel, Anne Valérie Hash, Christian Dior, Givenchy, Elie Saab, Alexis Mabille and Jean-Paul Gaultier.

For more information visit
WWW.MODEAPARIS.COM

Louis Vuitton and Lanvin. It is about reflecting on all that is beautiful in this world. It is about everything that is worth preserving and enjoying, every moment that is appreciated, every glass of wine and every sunny day.

No, it's not colorful. No, it's not bright or electric. It is subdued. It is calm but so powerful. Almost like a park on a sunny day, so peaceful with beauty resonating all around.

^THE CHANEL BOUTIQUE AT 31 RUE CAMBON

BAINS

NEIGHBORHOODS

PALAIS-ROYALE (1ST ARRONDISSEMENT)
The center of Paris: the Louvre, the Palais-Royale, the Tuileries Gardens and luxury shopping.

LE MARAIS (3RD)
A Right Bank neighborhood filled with beautiful young professionals, boutiques, bookstores and cafés.

LATIN QUARTER (5TH)
Home to the Sorbonne, students and a quiet, neighborhood feel.

SAINT-GERMAIN (6TH)
Upscale, classically bohemian Left Bank home of fashion's most famous hangouts and the Jardin du Luxembourg.

CHAMPS ELYSÉES/MADELINE (8TH)
A magical area of pure Parisian luxury: the Place de la Concorde and the ritzy Hotel Crillon.

PIGALLE (9TH)
Raunchy Pigalle is home to strip clubs and sex shops, plus underground labels and boutiques.

OBERKAMPF / BASTILLE (11TH)
Young and trendy with lots of cool bars and a slightly grungy feel.

MONTMARTRE (18TH)
Artsy and filled with tourists, but beautiful nonetheless. Home to the famous Moulin Rouge.

BELLEVILLE (20TH)
Outlying neighborhood filled with students, artists and young people; an exciting place for a night out on the town.

< A MONTMARTRE ALLEY

CAFÉ DE FLORE
A classic Parisian fashion hangout, featuring a sandwich named for Sonia Rykiel. Don't be surprised to see Karl Lagerfeld here.
172, boulevard Saint-Germain
6th Arrondissement, Paris
+33 (0) 1 45 44 33 40
WWW.CAFEDEFLORE.FR

BRASSERIE LIPP
Ultra expensive and exclusive, the place for Paris' fashion elite to see and be seen.
151, boulevard Saint-Germain
6th Arrondissement, Paris
+33 (0) 1 45 48 53 91

LE PROGRÈS
This Marais bistro is a favorite of Paris' new intellectual class, and its outdoor café boasts the city's most beautiful bobos.
1, rue de Bretagne
3rd Arrondissement, Paris
+33 (0) 1 42 72 01 44

HÔTEL AMOUR
This cheeky hotel was formerly a by-the-hour dive. Today it's a hip place for brunch or drinks.
8, rue Navarin
9th Arrondissement, Paris
+33 (0) 1 48 78 31 80
WWW.HOTELAMOURPARIS.FR

LE MONTANA
From the duo of André Saraiva and *Purple* editor Olivier Zahm, revived '60s club Le Montana has become the go-to place for sexy debauchery for fashion types and international celebs.
28, rue Saint-Benoît
6th Arrondissement, Paris
+33 (0) 1 42 22 46 03

< CAFÉ DE FLORE

THE CAPITAL OF COOL
COLETTE

Colette introduced a new way to shop when it opened its doors on the Right Bank in 1997. It's equal parts boutique and art gallery—and undoubtedly the world's premiere arbiter of cool. The mother-daughter team of Colette Roussaux and Sarah Lerfel runs the tri-level temple to good design, which features a carefully (and playfully) edited selection of the best in design from around the globe. Racks of clothing from cutting-edge labels Comme des Garçons and Maison Martin Margiela share the space with young, emerging and streetwear labels, plus an inspiring selection of books, music, magazines, limited-edition toys and even water.

With a constantly rotating selection, a trip to Colette is guaranteed to surprise and introduce shoppers to a hot new designer they haven't heard of yet—the store regularly partners with emerging designers for exhibitions and limited-edition pieces. Not only does a collab here offer instant international exposure, it's the equivalent of an official stamp of fashion-world approval.

Colette spokesperson Guillaume Salmon gave us the lowdown on store's unique take on Paris style.

∧ COLETTE'S RUE SAINT-HONORÉ STOREFRONT AND THE BOUTIQUE'S FIRST FLOOR

COLETTE CARRIES ALL TYPES OF
ITEMS, HOW ARE THEY SELECTED?
Guillaume Salmon: Colette is a famil-
ial and independent store, our buyer,
Sarah, is the daughter of Colette, and
she selects with the most simple rule of
the world: she selects what she likes!

HOW DO YOU CHOOSE WHICH DESIGN-
ERS/ARTISTS TO WORK WITH?
GS: The collaborations are made on
the same rule as the selection, and
when we have the opportunity to
make one, we do it with pleasure.
Or the brands ask us to do something and we say yes (or no), or we
propose (and they say yes or no).

COLETTE HAS BECOME THE ULTIMATE
SHOPPING DESTINATION IN PARIS, AND A
SYMBOL OF PARISIAN STYLE ITSELF. HOW
WOULD YOU DESCRIBE PARIS STYLE?
GS: I guess Paris style is as different
as there are some different areas, but
one thing maybe that's important
for the Parisian is to be able to get
this touch of style with a simple
and discreet sophistication.

COLETTE PARIS

213, rue Saint-Honoré
1st Arrondissement, Paris
+33 (0) 1 55 35 33 90
WWW.COLETTE.FR

THE EVERYMAN
RAD HOURANI

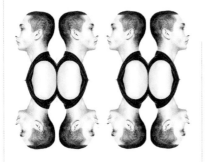

In an industry based on trends, Rad Hourani's sleek, monochromatic and unisex designs stand out. His vision is consistent, and entirely his own, each season an evolution of his previous work. The designer was born in Jordan, moved to Montreal in his teens and now splits his time between New York and Paris, giving Hourani a uniquely global view of fashion.

HOW WOULD YOU DESCRIBE THE RAD HOURANI LABEL? WHAT IS THE RAD HOURNAI LOOK?
Unisex, timeless, symmetric, straight, black, slick, geometric shapes, layered silhouettes that, by the use of fluid materials, come alive through the movement of the wearer.

WHAT TYPE OF PERSON IS THAT?
Someone who similarly appreciates the geometry of clothing and who under-stands there's a sensuality without relying on the human form. And of course, someone who's not trying to follow a trend. People who do not define themselves as men or women and who go beyond the classical demographical criteria.

DO YOU WEAR YOUR OWN DESIGNS? HOW DOES THAT INFLUENCE THE CLOTHES YOU MAKE?
I believe that using what I would like to wear as a starting point to the design process is the most truthful and straight-forward approach. So yes, I do. It allows me to stay focused on my aesthetic statement and also assess my commitment to wear-ability, functionality and comfort. I don't need to be the one who makes the boldest statement every season, I'd much rather commit to my personal aesthetics and that of the people who like to wear my clothes.

HOW DID YOU END UP CREATING CLOTHING THAT IS NOT DEFINED BY GENDER?
It never made sense to me when I saw dressing rules or codes between a male or a female. All my designs are made to be unisex. I am more attached to the notion of purity and by choosing black simple, stark lines, I strive to blur gender boundaries. Apparent simplic-ity with a refinement in details.

^ THE DESIGNER AND LOOKS FROM THE AUTUMN/WINTER 2010/2011 COLLECTION

I am interested in making things that make
me think and react, I like to do things in my
own way, I can't follow rules or do things
similar to everyone else. So for example
when I created the transformable jacket in
Collection #5, I liked the idea of making
a jacket that zips on and off in 50 different styles—by mixing fabrics and pieces.

**HOW DOES YOUR BACKGROUND AS A
STYLIST INFLUENCE YOUR WORK?**
Styling is great to learn how to use clothes
but, more importantly, if you have design
ambitions, it's a great way to analyze how
things are constructed and marketed,
especially for someone who never went
to design or fashion school, like me.

**YOU'VE LIVED ALL OVER THE WORLD. HOW
HAS TRAVEL INFLUENCED YOUR DESIGN?**

Circumstances have brought me to move
since an early point in my life. I have felt
compelled to continue doing this, as this
experience has made me consider things
with a wider perspective, with no restric-
tions. I want to convey this notion with
my line and design clothes that can be
worn by anyone, anywhere, anytime.

WHERE DO YOU CONSIDER HOME?
The Universe.

WHERE DO YOU GO TO FIND INSPIRATION?
Everywhere. In designing my collections,
I try to strip my sources of inspiration
of any obvious iconographic reference,
concentrating rather on their essential,
bare energy. I design from a virgin point
of view, trying to elude classical ready-to-
wear rules that make us believe that women
and men deserve different approaches.

For more on Rad Hourani visit
WWW.RADHOURANI.COM

AMBASSADORS OF THE AVANT-GARDE
ANDREA CREWS

Andrea Crews is a fashion label with a mission: fashion, art and activism. Led by Maroussia Rebecq, the collective transforms vintage and dead-stock clothing into new, one-of-a-kind pieces. They also stage elaborate performance pieces as an alternative to the fashion show—street protests, happenings and interactive presentations. In an industry full of champagne and air-kissing, Andrea Crews is putting the fun back in fashion.

Just in time for Paris Fashion Week in March 2010, the Crews crew took residency at the Centre Pompidou, where they reworked classically bourgeois French

brands including Moncler and Rossignol into new pieces with an edgier attitude and the Crews sense of humor. At the end of their stay, the group presented a fashion show that transformed the museum into a mountaintop scene, and ended with a spontaneous dance party.

The collective got its name when Rebecq moved to Paris after art school and wanted to promote her work. She created Andrea , Crews as her mouthpiece, a PR with an intentionally ambiguous name. (Is Andrea an Italian girl or a German boy? Is it Cruise like Tom, Cruz like Penélope or Crews like a group?) "Anyone can be Andrea Crews," says Rebecq, "All around the world."

Back at the label's studio, located among the sex shops and strip clubs of Pigalle, the Crews studio is filled with embellished Nikes and the boldy patterned Jogging Collection, featuring tracksuits covered in playful paisleys and floral prints.

A little bit hip-hop and entirely over the top—in the best way possible.

ANDREA CREWS STUDIO
10, rue Frochot
9th Arrondissement, Paris
WWW.ANDREACREWS.COM

SCENES FROM THE ANDREA CREWS
AUTUMN/WINTER 2010/2011 PRESENTATION

BELGIUM

In 1988, a group of six young designers from Antwerp's Royal Academy of Fine Arts piled into a van, drove to London and burst onto the fashion scene. Together, Ann Demeulemeester, Dries Van Noten, Walter Van Beirendonck, Dirk Van Saene, Dirk Bikkembergs and Marina Yee offered a brand-new vision, a sophisticated take on fashion that had more in common with the Japanese avant-garde than with other European deisngers.

Of the six, only Demeulemeester, Van Noten and Van Beirendonck continue to show in Paris. And each season, fashion followers look particularly forward to Demeulemeester's tailored and dramatic collections, and Van Noten's innovative treatment of prints and textures.

Since the so-called Antwerp Six first made their debut, the city has continued to produce some of fashion's most exciting and intellectual designers, though some Belgian designers, such as

Martin Margiela, a contemporary of the original Antwerp Six, choose to relocate to Paris (where most of Antwerp's designers show).

By the late 1990s, a second wave of Belgians began making waves in the fashion scene. These designers, including Raf Simons, An Vandervorst and Filip Arickx of A.F. Vandevorst and Véronique Leroy (as well the new-defunct labels Veronique Branquinho and Bruno Pieters) continued the Antwerp tradition of cerebral and serious fashion.

By the early 21st century, fashion found a wunderkind in yet another Belgian designer, Brussles-born Olivier Theyskens. Before he was 25, Theyskens had dressed Madonna in his own dark-edged designs and rocketed to fame. This led to a position at French house Rochas, where his demicouture creations won critical acclaim, but proved too precious for retail. He later moved on to Nina Ricci before partnering with sportswear label Theory in 2010.

ANN DEMEULEMEESTER
Careful tailoring and a minimalist palette of black and white make each Ann Demeulemeester collection a classic—with a subtly gothic twist, and the type of relaxed layering that fashion crowd loves.
Ann Demeulemeester
Leopold de Waelplaats
Antwerp, Belgium
+32 (0) 3 216 01 33
WWW.ANNDEMEULEMEESTER.BE

DRIES VAN NOTEN
Eclectic use of color, ethnic- and art-inspired pattern, and careful layering have become the signatures of Dries Van Noten ever since his first menswear collection was bought up by Barneys in 1986—and sold in the women's department.
Nationalestraat 16
Antwerp, Belgium
+32 (0) 3 470 25 10
WWW.DRIESVANNOTEN.BE

WALTER VAN BEIRENDONCK
One of Belgium's more eccentric talents, Van Beirendonck creates bold and colorful collections with a sense of humor.
Sint-Antoniusstraat 12
Antwerp, Belgium
+32 (0) 3 213 26 44
WWW.WALTERVANBEIRENDONCK.COM

AF VANDEVORST
Designers An Vandervorst and Filip Arickx design deconstructed, architectural garments inspired by conceptual art and philosophy. Their intellectual designs lie on the borders of art and fashion, of sculpture and wearable clothing.
WWW.AFVANDEVORST.BE

HAIDER ACKERMANN
Haider Ackermann was born in Colombia and studied at Antwerp's Royal Academy of Fine Arts before launching his own line. One of fashion's most exciting young designers, he has found a following for his severe cuts, languid dresses and covetable draped leather jackets.
WWW.HAIDERACKERMANN.BE

RAF SIMONS
Self-taught fashion designer Raf Simons worked in furniture design before launching his menswear collection. Since then he's become a leading figure in men's fashion for his slim, sleek suits and anti-establishment attitude towards the fashion business. In 2005 he was named creative director for Jil Sander, wowing critics with his perfectly minimal creations.
WWW.RAFSIMONS.COM
WWW.JILSANDER.COM

THE ICONS

CHANEL

The House of Chanel was founded by Coco Chanel in 1909, offering practical, menswear-inspired clothing for modern women. Today, Karl Lagerfeld, one of the last of the great couturiers, keeps Chanel's vision alive with modern and luxurious interpretations of her classic suits and tweeds, plus couture gowns.

31, rue Cambon
1st Arrondissement, Paris
+33 (0) 1 42 86 28 00
WWW.CHANEL.COM

CHRISTIAN DIOR

Christian Dior revolutionized fashion with the exaggerated femininity of his New Look of 1947. Today, designer John Galliano continues Dior's legacy in both ready-to-wear and couture. Galliano's whimsical and chic creations reference fashion history in delightfully theatrical ways, while retaining the label's womanly allure.

30, Avenue Montaigne
8th Arrondissement, Paris
+33 (0) 1 40 73 73 73
WWW.DIOR.COM

CHANEL
HAUTE COUTURE

CHRISTIAN DIOR
HAUTE COUTURE

JEAN-PAUL GAULTIER

The designer who famously created Madonna's cone bra has played with fashion's boundaries since the beginning of his career, exploring ideas of gender and sexuality with his clothing. Since then he's made waves for his original ready-to-wear and couture, perfectly executed and always *trés* French.

44, avenue George V
8th Arrondissement, Paris
+33 (0) 1 44 43 00 44
WWW.JEANPAULGAULTIER.COM

YVES SAINT LAURENT

Yves Saint Laurent took over Dior at just 21. He shook the fashion world—first, with his trapeze dresses and later, by making ready-to-wear fashionable under his own label. Today the house is helmed by Stefano Pilati, who, like Saint Laurent, creates strong and sexy clothing on trend and on fashion's cutting edge.

6, Place Saint Sulpice
6th Arrondissement, Paris
+ 33 (0) 1 43 29 43 00
WWW.YSL.COM

JEAN-PAUL GAULTIER
HAUTE COUTURE

YVES SAINT
LAURENT

LES CLASSIQUES

BALENCIAGA

Since the late 1990s, designer Nicolas Ghesquière has breathed new life into the classic maison, pioneering a futuristic look of space-age shapes and innovative material, plus the best accessories around. **WWW.BALENCIAGA.COM**

BALMAIN

It's grungy glamour with lots of va-va-voom—skin-tight dresses, ripped Ts that costs thousands and low-slung leather pants—at Christophe Decarnin's Balmain. **WWW.BALMAIN.COM**

CÉLINE

Phoebe Philo creates sharp and modern clothing that sophisticated women want to wear: subtly sexy and totally grown-up. **WWW.CELINE.COM**

CHLOÉ

Chloé's refined feminine dressing features classic shapes—the perfect pant, the perfect blouse, the perfect coat—in creamy colors. **WWW.CHLOE.COM**

GIVENCHY

Riccardo Tisci, one of fashion's most adventurous designers, has brought high-tech prints, bold gold jewelry and towering heels to the house best known for the "little black dress." **WWW.GIVENCHY.COM**

JOHN GALLIANO

John Galliano is as dramatic, imaginative and fiercely original as his clothing. His collections combine historical and ethnic references, transporting viewers to another world completely his own. **WWW.JOHNGALLIANO.COM**

CHLOÉ

KENZO

KENZO

Kenzo Takada was one of the first Japanese designers to show abroad. Thirty years later, the label is totally Parisian. **WWW.KENZO.COM**

LANVIN

At Paris' oldest fashion house, Alber Ebaz creates flowing gowns and vibrant cocktail dresses that are the epitome of well-crafted luxury. **WWW.LANVIN.COM**

LOUIS VUITTON

Marc Jacobs brought the luxury label into the 21st century with ready-to-wear and collaborations with artists such as Richard Prince and Takashi Murakami. Its accessories are world famous, but it's the label's refined luxury and Jacobs' playful spirit that keep the fashion crowd interested. **WWW.LOUISVUITTON.COM**

NINA RICCI

Filling the formidable and fashion-forward shoes of Olivier Theyskens, newcomer Peter Copping has returned the house to understated, underwhelming elegance. **WWW.NINARICCI.COM**

ROCHAS

Italian designer Marco Zanini is the latest to head the historic Parisian fashion house, experimenting with print, color and ladylike sportswear in his early collections with the label. **WWW.ROCHAS.COM**

SONIA RYKIEL

Paris' famously red-tressed designer is known for her boldly striped knits and playful take on fashion, including a slightly eccentric Left Bank style of shrunken and oversized shapes. **WWW.SONIARYKIEL.FR**

STORES

BALENCIAGA
10, Avenue George V
8th Arron., Paris
+33 (0) 1 47 20 21 11

BALMAIN
44, rue François 1er
8th Arron., Paris
+33 (0) 1 47 20 35 34

CÉLINE
36, Avenue Montaigne
8th Arron., Paris
+33 (0) 1 56 89 07 91

CHLOÉ
44, Avenue Montaigne
8th Arron., Paris
+33 (0) 1 47 23 0008

GIVENCHY
28, rue du Faubourg Saint-Honoré
8th Arron., Paris
+33 (0) 1 42 68 31 00

JOHN GALLIANO
384 rue Saint-Honoré
1st Arron., Paris
+33 (0) 1 55 35 40 40

KENZO
3, place des Victoires
1st Arron., Paris
+33 (0) 1 40 39 72 03

LANVIN
22, rue du Faubourg Saint-Honré
8th Arron., Paris
+33 (0) 1 44 71 31 73

LOUIS VUITTON
101, avenue des Champs-Elysées
8th Arron., Paris
+33 (0) 1 53 57 52 00

NINA RICCI
39, avenue Montaigne
8th Arron., Paris

SONIA RYKIEL
175, boulevard Saint-Germain
6th Arron., Paris
+33 (0) 1 49 54 60 60

THE INDEPENDENTS

ALEXIS MABILLE

A young designer with a fresh take on haute couture—and a resume that includes YSL and Dior—Alexis Mabille adds a shock of color to the sometimes subtle Parisian catwalks with his sharply tailored pieces.

WWW.ALEXISMABILLE.COM

ANNE VALÉRIE HASH

A young and independent designer offering both ready-to-wear and haute couture, Parisian-born Anne Valérie Hash has created her own unique brand of wearable couture.

WWW.A-V-H.COM

DAMIR DOMA

Croatian-born designer Damir Doma cut his teeth working under Raf Simons. On his own since 2006, Doma's signature line rides on fashion's dark wave, with designs that range from the ethereal to the monastic.

WWW.DAMIRDOMA.COM

GASPARD YURKIEVICH

Gaspard Yurkievich creates contemporary, urban clothing with a dark edge

WWW.GASPARDYURKIEVICH.COM

ISABEL MARANT

French women swear by Isabel Marant's perfectly wearable and distinctly French clothing for effortless bohemian style.

WWW.ISABELMARANT.TM.FR

MAISON MARTIN MARGIELA

The enigmatic designer may have left his signature label, but Maison Martin Margiela continues to push the boundaries of fashion with clever conceptual pieces as well as perfectly minimal basics.

WWW.MAISONMARTINMARGIELA.COM

MARTIN GRANT

Australian import Martin Grant makes power dressing easy, with key pieces—leather dresses, sharp

DAMIR DOMA

GASPARD YURKIEVICH

MAISON MARTIN MARGIELA

jackets and tailored trousers—that transition seamlessly from boardroom to evening.
WWW.MARTINGRANTPARIS.COM

RAD HOURANI
Minimalist, monochromatic and totally unisex, Rad Hourani's clothing is meant to last season after season, totally unaffected by trends. **WWW.RADHOURANI.COM**

RICK OWENS
American expat Rick Owens is an avant-garde designer with a cult-like following. His signature look is draped, layered and asymmetrical in black and grays, plus lots of fur and the best leather jackets in the biz. **WWW.RICKOWENS.EU**

VIKTOR & ROLF
Dutch duo Viktor Horsting and Rolf Snoeren are fashion's mad scientists. Their out-there clothing has included 3D letters built into coats, layers upon layers of the same garment and full dresses with chunks cut out. **WWW.VIKTOR-ROLF.COM**

STORES

DAMIR DOMA
6, rue des Arquebusiers
3rd Arrondissement, Paris
+33 (0) 1 45 27 09 30

GASPARD YURKIEVICH
43, rue Charlot
3rd Arrondissement, Paris
+33 (0)1 42 77 42 48

ISABEL MARANT
47, rue Saintonge
3rd Arrondissement, Paris
+33 01 42 78 19 24

MAISON MARTIN MARGIELA
25 bis, rue de Montpensier
1st Arrondissement, Paris
+33 (0)1 40 15 07 55

MARTIN GRANT
10, rue Charlot
3rd Arrondissement, Paris
+33 (0)1 42 71 39 49

RICK OWENS
Jardins Du Palais Royal
130-133 Galerie de Valois
1st Arrondissement, Paris
+33 (0)1 40 20 42 52

MARTIN GRANT

RICK OWENS

VIKTOR & ROLF

CONTEMPORARY SHOPPING GUIDE

A.P.C.

Independent of current trends, Jean Touitou creates classic pieces that are made to last and never go out of style. The label has found a cult following for its sweet summer dresses, slim-cut suits and top-quality denim.

WWW.APC.FR

HEIMSTONE

At first glance, Heimstone is a line of simple, girly designs, but upon closer inspection the label reveals subtle but edgy details such as studs and stones. The result is a collection that's feminine, but not too sweet.

WWW.HEIMSTONE.COM

MAJE

Sophisticated, chic and just a bit fashion-forward, Judith Milgrom's Maje is grown-up and wearable.

WWW.MAJE-PARIS.FR

PAUL & JOE

Since 1995 Sophie Albou has cornerd the market on slightly bohemian, seriously Parisian threads, expanding her label around the globe.

WWW.PAULANDJOE.COM

SANDRO

Fun, young pieces for instant mix-and-match style.

WWW.SANDRO-PARIS.COM

HEIMSTONE

PAUL & JOE

STORES

THE KOOPLES

Blazers, brogues, or button-ups, The Kooples is the ultimate destination for bobo basics. In addition to their line of preppy pieces with a little rock 'n' roll edge, the brand has the cutest ad campaigns in the biz. As a play on the brand's name, their ads features a real-life couple.

WWW.THEKOOPLES.COM

ZADIG & VOLTAIRE

All the basics a cool girl needs for a truly Parisian wardrobe. Need proof? "It" actress Joséphine de la Baume stars in the label's campaigns.

WWW.ZADIG-ET-VOLTAIRE.COM

A.P.C.
5, rue de Marseille
10th Arrondissement, Paris
+33 (0)1 42 39 84 46

HEIMSTONE
23, rue du Cherche-Midi
6th Arron., Paris
+33 (0) 1 45 49 15 73

MAJE
16, rue Montmartre
1st Arron., Paris
+33 (0) 1 42 36 36 75

PAUL & JOE
2, avenue Montaigne
8th Arron., Paris
+33 (0) 1 47 20 57 50

SANDRO
7, rue Montpensier
1st Arron., Paris
+33 (0) 1 40 15 09 51

THE KOOPLES
191, rue Saint-Honoré
1st Arron., Paris
+33 (0) 1 49 26 05 35

ZADIG & VOLTAIRE
18-20 rue François 1er
1st Arron., Paris
+33 (0) 1 40 70 97 89

THE KOOPLES

ZADIG & VOLTAIRE

MILAN

1865 Construction begins on Galleria Vittorio Emanuele II, one
of Milan's most luxurious shopping destinations

1913 Mario Prada establishes the Prada leather goods store

1951 Giovanni Battista Giorgini hosts Italy's first fashion show at his home

1977 Fendi launches its ready-to-wear line

1979 Milan Fashion Week is established

1990 10 Corso Como opens as a bookstore and gallery

1991 Gianni Versace creates his iconic Warhol dress for Versace Couture

1994 Tom Ford is appointed creative director of Gucci

1995 Gucci becomes a publicly traded company

2008 Valentino retires after 45 years in the business

2009 *Vogue Italia* makes waves with a ground-breaking
issue featuring only black models

MILAN: MADE IN ITALY

BY FABIANA FIEROTTI AND ILARIA NORSA

If Milan has a bad reputation, perhaps it's because the city is full of contradictions. Its buildings are low and brown, not much to look at. And yet, behind each doorway lies a cozy tavern, a luxurious boutique, a lushly landscaped courtyard, or a home decked out in cutting-edge modern design. You just have to know where to look.

For the first-time visitor, Milan is difficult to navigate and sometimes hard to understand. It takes time, or a knowing guide, to discover the beauty that the city has to offer.

Milan doesn't look like one of the world's reigning fashion capitals at first glance. The city is Italy's financial hub and the banker look rules the streets: perfectly tailored suits, driving shoes, khakis and cardigans. However, this is Italy, and a premium is placed on quality and fit. Even the most conservative look is done with an eye for style.

For the fashion-savvy visitor to Milan, it's a stark contrast to the luxurious glamour and raw sex appeal exported by Italy's runways in recent decades.

But Italy's affair with fashion runs much deeper than that. It is based on a tradition of craftsmanship. In fact, many of Italy's most famous

^ A LOOK FROM FEBRUARY'S SPRING/SUMMER 2010 COLLECTION WWW.FEBRUARY.IT
< (PREVIOUS SPREAD) GRAFFITI ON THE CORSO DI PORTA TICINESE

labels got their start as luxury goods companies. Fendi, now the Italian home of designer Karl Lagerfeld, began as a furrier in Rome in 1925. Prada dates back even further. Founded by Mario Prada in 1913 as a leather goods shop, it remained a leather company until Mario's granddaughter, Miuccia

Prada, joined the company in 1978. She expanded the Prada label to include bags, then shoes, and, finally, ready-to-wear in 1989.

As Italy's heritage brands branched out into clothing, once-tired labels became fashionable yet again. With the appearance of the phrase "made

^ TICINESE BOUTIQUES MY CLOSET (ABOVE) AND OSKLEN

in Italy" in the 1980s, the labels gave a boost to the national economy, thanks to the quality of craftsmanship, efficient manufacturing and sophisticated commercial skills of the Italian fashion system.

The '80s was also the decade of Giorgio Armani. The designer epitomized '80s excess with power suits fit for kings of finance and ultra-expensive gowns for A-list celebrities. Through licensing and perfumes, he expanded his label into one of the world's largest fashion empires.

By the 1990s, Gianni Versace was the new face of Italian fashion. His label was the perfect uniform for the decade's reigning supermodel beauties: bold and brash with lots of logos printed on expensive fabrics. Throughout the decade, designers at Italy's famed houses—siblings Gianni and Donatella at Versace; American Tom Ford at Gucci; Domenico Dolce and Stefano Gabbana; Roberto Cavalli—pushed necklines lower and hemlines higher, culminating in Jennifer Lopez's famous barely-there, jungle-print Versace at the 2000 Grammy Awards. Ten years and a global financial crisis later, such outsized glamour seems out of touch.

Louche luxury is not all that the city has to offer, though. Prada maintains its intellectual bent,

REQUIRED READING

VOGUE ITALIA
This boundary-pushing member of the *Vogue* family features regular contributions from photographer Steven Meisel. **WWW.VOGUE.IT**

PIG MAGAZINE
Indie and irreverent, *PIG* magazine is the voice of young Milan. **WWW.PIGMAG.COM**

SWIDE
The online mag from Dolce&Gabbana features interviews with leading fashion figures. **WWW.SWIDE.COM**

COLORS
Founded by Benetton, *COLORS* takes an intelligent view of world culture. **WWW.COLORSMAGAZINE.COM**

ALL THE PRETTY BIRDS
Milanese street style captured by the lens of photog Tamu McPherson. **WWW.ALLTHEPRETTYBIRDS.BLOGSPOT.COM**

URBAN
Cultural dispatches from cities around the world. **WWW.URBANMAGAZINE.IT**

DIEDLASTNIGHT
Music, party coverage and street style from Milan's indie scene. **WWW.DIEDLASTNIGHT.COM**

creating collections that are favorites among fashion editors and shoppers alike. Sure, it's expensive, but this is the kind of fashion that pushes ideas forward. And then there's Missoni, a third-generation family business based on knitwear with a luxe bohemian sensibility.

Even though select labels continue to be editorial favorites, Milan's status as a fashion capital is being challenged, for, what feels like, the first time. American *Vogue* editor, Anna Wintour, made waves when she only attended three days of the city's Fashion Week in February 2010. That same season, Cathy Horyn at the *New York Times* complained of "an eternity of bad clothes crammed into four days." After vanguard Tom Ford's departure from Gucci in 2006, Horyn wrote, the city feels lost.

This is an opportunity, however, for Italy's young creatives to find their voice. Fashion here was once something related only to a small bunch of powerful names, handed down from generation to generation or learned only by spending years in the most well known maisons.

Today, more people are breaking into the Italian fashion industry on their own merits. Young brands such as FEBRUARY, which adds a bit of edge to sophisticated Italian style

MY CLOSET, CORSO DI PORTA TICINESE >

in its incredibly wearable designs. And there are others, including streetwear label VNGRD, which takes cues from hip-hop and the underground; ultra-hip sunglasses brand Retrosuperfuture, which makes modern and original frames; plus Pharmacy and many others. They all started from zero and really made it.

It is all about an underground scene that has always existed, in a certain way, in Milan. Of course, uptown you had luxury, pomp, exclusive restaurants and exclusive parties for exclusive people, but the city also boasted very big punk and New Wave scenes that served as precursors to today's street and indie fashion scenes.

To explore this side of Milan you'll need to look past the luxurious shopping of the ritzy Quadrilatero della Moda to the vintage shops and nightclubs along the Navigli, to the rock 'n' roll boutiques of Ticinese and beyond. This is the young Milan, the city at its most irreverent. The Milan filled with designers, PR reps and journalists, all melted together by the passion for an uncommon sense of fashion, for fresh ideas and new concepts.

Creativity is the keyword.

10 CORSO COMO

So much more than just a department store, 10 Corso Como is a landmark of good taste, featuring a café, gallery and even a three-room hotel, all set in a traditional Milanese palazzo. Founded by Carla Sozzani—publisher, gallerist and sister of *Vogue Italia* editor Franca Sozzani—it's based on the concept of "slow shopping", an adaptation of Italy's Slow Food movement that's all about taking the time to enjoy the moment. At 10 Corso Como, shoppers enter through a lush courtyard and into a fantasy world. It's a place to meet friends and relax, and a place to get inspired.

And then, of course, there's the shopping—all the world's top labels from Alaïa to Z, plus cute accessories, books and quirky gifts. If your budget doesn't allow for designer shopping, grab a seat in the café, home to some of the most stylish people-watching the city has to offer.

Corso Como, 10
Milan
+39 (0) 2 290 02674
WWW.10CORSOCOMO.COM

YOUNG MILAN

To enjoy Milan, you need to see it like a local. Fabiana Fierotti and Ilaria Norsa of Milan's most exciting independent publication, *PIG* Magazine, hunted down nine tastemakers for their take on Italy's fashion capital.

LUCIO VANOTTI

Fashion designer, FEBRUARY

WWW.FEBRUARY.IT

FAVORITE SHOPPING AREA
Brera

FAVORITE SHOPS
Frip (Corso di Porta Ticinese, 16)
FEBRUARY (Via Arena, 19)
Jil Sander (Via Pietro Verri, 6)

FLEA MARKET
Piazzale Cuoco every Sunday morning

VINTAGE
Bonfante (Via San Gregorio)

INSIDER TIP
Follow a cool, elderly, bourgeois Milanese to discover the city's well-kept secrets.

SIDNEY GEUBELLE

Model from Belgium,
in love with Milan.

FAVORITE AREAS
Navigli and Ticinese

VINTAGE
- Humana Vintage
  (Via Cappellari, 3)
- Lipstick Vintage (Corso
  Garibaldi, 79), where you can also
  rent clothes just for one night!
- Ripa di Porta Ticinese is perfect for a
  nice walk and some vintage shopping.
- For amazing vintage sunglasses you can't
  miss Foto Veneta Ottica (Via Torino, 57).

FLEA MARKET
San Donato every Sunday morning;
Senigallia (Via Valenza) every Saturday.

MILAN TOP 3
1. Cycling through Milan and passing by
   Castello Sforzesco and Parco Sempione.
   Especially at night, when the streets
   are empty, coming back from parties
   with loud music ringing in my ears.
2. The Bruttoposse party, really my favorite
   night of the week! Super chill and
   easy people; it's full of good vibes.
3. €1 shops: I love to buy things I will
   never use just because it's cheap.

GIACOMO PIAZZA

247 Showroom, Volta Footwear

WWW.247SHOWROOM.IT
WWW.VOLTAFOOTWEAR.IT

FAVORITE AREA
Brera (shopping), Ticinese (nightlife)

FLEA MARKET
Antiques Flea Market every last
Sunday of the month on the Navigli.

FAVORITE SHOPS
- Antonia Man (Via Ponte Vetero, 9)
- Cargo High Tech (Via Privata
  Antonio Meucci, 39)
- Bookstore/Magazines: 10 Corso
  Como (Corso Como, 10)

MILAN TOP 3
1. Cycling over Navigli during springtime.
2. Eating bio food at Lattughino
   (Via Andrea Ponti, 1)
3. Having a coffee at Fioraio
   Bianchi (Via Montebello, 7)

MARCELO BURLON

Editor, DJ, PR and Party Instigator. The "Mayor of the county of Milan."

MARCELOBURLONENTERPRISE.COM

FAVORITE AREAS
Ticinese and Navigli

MILAN TOP 3
1. Having tea on the Rinascente's rooftop terrace overlooking the Duomo (La Rinascente; Piazza del Duomo)
2. A bowling match in the outskirts of the city (Bowling dei Fiori; Via Renzo e Lucia, 4)
3. A pool match in Porta Genova (EuroJolly Biliardo; Corso Cristoforo Colombo, 13)

HOT PARTIES
- Pink is Punk, my party every Friday night at Magazzini Generali (Via Pietrasanta, 14)
- Bruttoposse, every Thursday at La Sacrestia (Via Conchetta, 20)
- Plastic Club, every Friday, Saturday and Sunday (Viale Umbria, 120)

EDWARD BUCHANAN

Fashion design consultant and creative director of SANSOVINO 6

WWW.SANSOVINO6.IT

VINTAGE
Vintage military, which you can find all over the Navigli area.

HAIRDRESSER
Franco (Via Lecco 5) is the best old-school haircutter I know! A chic and classic salon for buzz cuts and fades.

WELL KEPT SECRET
Sabrina Restaurant (Piazza XXIV Maggio). A full-course meal for around €11! It is easy, good, unpretentious and very unglamorous.

MILAN TOP 3
1. Dinner at Christian e Armando (Sardinian cuisine) with the extended family (Corso Cristoforo Colombo, 10).
2. A breeze through Antonioli to see what's new.
3. Summer strolls on Porta Ticinese and laying in the sun at Parco Sempione.

FACE A.K.A. LUCIANO SERPI (180GR)

DJ, Graphic Designer, Chef

FAVORITE AREA
Ticinese

MILAN TOP 3

1. A "panzerotto" at Luini's
(Via Santa Radegonda, 16)

2. Records at Serendeepity's
(Corso di Porta Ticinese, 100)

3. Happy hour at Rita's
(Via Angelo Fumagalli, 1)

FEDERICA ZAMBON

Manager, WOK

VIA COL DI LANA 5/A
WWW.WOK-STORE.COM

BEST SHOPPING AREA
Garibaldi

VINTAGE
The two crazy girls in Ripa di Porta
Ticinese…the shop has no name, you'll find
it on the Naviglio Ripa di Porta Ticinese.

MILAN TOP 3
1. Have a walk in the park
2. Shop at Prada (Via Montenapoleone 19)
3. Break at Cucchi (Corso Genova, 1)

FEDERICA DE CARLO

PR for Slam Jam, spinner

BEST SHOPPING

In the end I yield to the Fashion Quadrilateral: Via Montenapoleone, Via della Spiga, Corso Venezia and Via Sant'Andrea.

___

FAVORITE SHOPS

- Antonia Boutique (Via Ponte Vetero, 1)
- Stussy Store (Corso di Porta Ticinese, 103)
- Slamjam Store (Via Pasquale Paoli, 3/5)

___

BRUNCH

Al Garghet (Via Selvanesco, 36)
It is not the proper place to brunch, since it's more of a traditional Milanese restaurant, but I love to go there with my friends, especially on Sunday.

WELL KEPT SECRET

A unique place to enjoy "pizzette" for lunch and the best gin and tonic in the city, it's in San Vittore neighborhood...go and search for it!

___

MILAN TOP 3

- Sunday, noon: Cucchi's daiquiri (Corso Genova, 1)
- Cycling among the alleys to Duomo.
- The entire tour on Tram 29.

GAIA VENUTI

Vintage Collector and Stylist

FAVORITE AREA

Ticinese

___

FAVORITE SHOP

10 Corso Como (Corso Como, 10)

___

VINTAGE

Vintage Delirium by Franco Jacassi (Via Sacchi, 3)

MILAN TOP 3

1. Breakfast at Clivati (Viale Coni Zugna, 57)
2. Shopping at Miu Miu (Via Sant'Andrea, 21) and Hermès (Via Sant'Andrea, 11)
3. The hamburgers at Margy's (Margy Burger; Piazza Santo Stefano) then off to the pole dance course.

DESIGN WEEK

While Milan has a reputation for being a sleepy city, every April it comes alive for the Salone Internazionale del Mobile, the annual Furniture Festival. More than 250,000 people from all over the world descend on the city, making it one of the most exciting times of the year to experience Milan.

I Salone is the world's largest design trade show, and it spills onto the city's streets with free and alternative events spread throughout the city.

While the main action is held at the FieraMilano complex in nearby Rho, those wanting a taste of the festival should head to Via Tortona, where many shops open their doors with special exhibitions, and often free champagne. Also, check out the universities, which often host free events showcasing young designers.

For more on Design Week in Milan visit **WWW.COSMIT.IT**

DESIGN WEEK CROWDS ON VIA TORTONA ^
THE INTERNI THINK TANK AT UNIVERSITA DEGLI STUDI DI MILANO ^

^ (FROM TOP) INTERNI THINK TANK;
NEW DESIGNS FROM ZONA TORTONA FESTIVAL CIRCUIT

NEIGHBORHOODS

QUADRILATERO DELLA MODA
The fashion rectangle—defined by the streets of Via Montenapoleone, Via Manzoni, Corso Venezia, and Via della Spiga—makes up Milan's most glittering shopping district, with big names such as Prada, Armani and Valentino alongside foreign labels such as Chanel and Christian Dior.

BRERA
Fashionable Brera is filled with boutiques, outdoor cafés and design stores. And as the home of the Accademia d'Arte, the neighborhood has a youthful, creative energy.

PORTA TICINESE
Quirky boutiques and vintage shops with rock 'n' roll attitude line the streets of this historic area named for its famous arch.

NAVIGLI
The picturesque canals of Navigli are lined with vintage and antique shops, street markets, as well as popular restaurants and nightspots.

GARIBALDI
Located near the city's growing business district, the area is home to the posh department store 10 Corso Como.

ISOLA
An under-the-radar neighborhood offering nice boutiques and an array of ethnic restaurants.

BOVISA
Bovisa is home to the Politecnico di Milano, a university specializing in science, technology and design, as well as to a wide variety of antique shopping.

< THE NAVIGLIO GRANDE

HOTSPOTS

GIACOMO BISTROT
Fashion folks go to see and be seen at the classic, French-inspired Giacomo Bistro.
Via Pasquale Sottocorno, 6
Milan
+39 (0) 2 760 233 13
WWW.GIACOMOMILANO.COM

BULGARI HOTEL
The garden of this luxurious hotel is a stylish destination for a light meal after a relaxing morning at the spa.
Via Privata Fratelli Gabba, 7/b
Milan
+39 (0) 2 805 805 1
WWW.BULGARIHOTELS.COM

PRAVDA VODKA BAR
Pravda is home to cold Russian vodka and hot bartenders.
Via Vittadini 6
Milan
WWW.MYSPACE.COM/PRAVDAMILANO

MORGAN'S
Cocktail bar Morgan's is old-school Italian: charming décor, photos of regulars on the walls and excellent service. Both the local students and an upscale bohemian crowd come for the food and the signature Vodka Daisy.
Via Novati, 2
Milan
+39 (0) 2 867 694

TAVERNA MORIGGI
An old-school taverna for traditional Milanese wine and cheese.
Via Morigi, 8
Milan
+39 (0) 2 805 820 07
WWW.TAVERNAMORIGGI.IT

< THE GARDEN AT BULGARI HOTEL

AN AMERICAN IN MILAN
TAMU MCPHERSON

Since moving from New York to Milan in 2005, Tamu McPherson has snapped the city's most stylish residents, and learned a thing or two about the local look. In 2008 she started her blog, All the Pretty Birds, with the idea: "Wherever we fall on the fashion spectrum, we are all beautiful creatures. We are all pretty birds."

HOW DID YOU GET YOUR STARTED SHOOTING STREET STYLE?
In 2006 I met an editor who I still work with, his name is Luca Lanzoni. Glamour.it had just started a street style community blog and he asked me to set the tone for the blog. Because it is a community and anyone can post, he wanted someone who had an eye for style, who would actually go out and shoot people.
I fell in love with it, because it allowed me to work with fashion all the time, every day, all day long. I see how the trends are interpreted on the streets and how they've trickled down. I see whispers of trends to come. It's a lot of fun, especially during fashion shows because you get to see the best-dressed people in the world, the fashion leaders.

FASHION BLOGS HAVE EXPLODED IN RECENT YEARS. HOW HAVE THINGS CHANGED SINCE YOU STARTED?
People take style into their own hands now. They want to be on top of the trends, so they'll take a piece from a collection like Balmain, and they'll try to recreate, even push it further and personalize it. More people can play.

HOW WOULD YOU DESCRIBE MILAN STYLE?
Milan style is very elegant; it's very chic. They are very well put together and regardless of the season they have a formula. In the summertime they have their color combinations that work well. If they're going to wear a pant, and a cardigan and a shirt, it's always really coordinated, really well; they don't really push the extremes too much. There is the base, and everybody falls back on that base. Same thing in the winter.

They have the best outerwear and they know how to coordinate their outerwear. If they do browns, they do browns, but everything is perfection, really beautiful.

HAVE YOU PICKED UP ANY STYLE TIPS?
The way I look at Milanese fashion, when you move to a foreign country you can't fight the system, you've got to understand it. It's not my style, but I really appreciate Milanese style and I use it when I need to. One of the best things is, if you have a base and you're having one of those days—"where do I go with this?"—and you just start at a base, it just makes it so much easier.

WHAT TYPE OF PEOPLE DO YOU PHOTOGRAPH?
I photograph a lot of students. Men I do photograph, but the women not so much. The atmosphere is kind of closed. It's not so easy to photograph a woman

that's well dressed, because she might not want to do it. So I photograph people who are students, who work in fashion, who are a little bit younger. I observe the more formal, the more elegant style every day, but I don't photograph it as much.

WHO ARE THE COOL KIDS NOW?

The cool kids in Milan are the students who attend Marangoni University or Istituto Europeo di Design, they're majoring in fashion design, they're majoring in styling, and they're super cool. Some of them attend school and they're promoters for parties. They have these nights with themes and they show up dressed based on the theme. They get really creative. They're doing the looks that came out of Paris: They were doing goth-inspired looks; they did their '80s. They're completely on-trend and they do it all the way.

There's this one girl I love to shoot and one day I saw her in a fur chubby [jacket] with neon-green Doc Martens, patent leather. And it was very cool because she was walking across Piazza della Scala, going to school.

THAT'S INTERESTING. THERE'S THE PERCEPTION THAT ITALIAN FASHION IS VERY LABEL-DRIVEN.

They are driven by tradition. And part of their tradition is they shop at certain places. I go to an open-air market on Mondays, and

I see women of all economic backgrounds at this place. You'll see a Birkin bag go up to one of these stands and buy her underwear. It's a tradition: Where do I get my good underwear and my good underclothes? At the open-air market they sell fish and they sells cheese, but theses women will buy their fish, they'll buy their cheese and they'll pick up a cashmere sweater. There's definitely a mix. It is all born in tradition, but they know, and they pick and choose.

See Tamu McPherson's shots of Milan's most stylish at
ALLTHEPRETTYBIRDS.BLOGSPOT.COM

TAMU'S PICKS

BOUTIQUES

ANTONIOLI
Cutting-edge international
brands including Rick Owens,
Ann Demeulemeester and
Maison Martin Margiela.
Via P. Paoli 1
Milan
+39 (0) 2 365 66494
WWW.ANTONIOLI.EU

FRIP
An edgy boutique featuring
international labels such as Acne,
Marios and Bernhard Willhelm,
plus music and magazines.
Corso di Porta Ticinese, 16
Milan
+39 (0) 2 83 21360
WWW.FRIP.IT

BANNER
Carries an elegant collection, including
designers Dries Van Noten, Stella
McCartney and Marc Jacobs.
Via Sant'Andrea 8
Milan
+39 (0) 2 760 04609

ANTONIA
A super-chic and glamorous Brera
boutique with Bottega Venetta, Balmain,
Lanvin and tons of killer accessories.
Via Ponte Vetero 1
Milan
+39 (0) 2 869 98340
WWW.ANTONIA.IT

RESTAURANTS/CAFES

FIORAIO BIANCHI
A bistro-style Brera restaurant
at a former florist.
Via Montebello, 7
Milan
+39 (0) 2 290 14390
WWW.FIORAIOBIANCHICAFFE.IT

N'OMBRA DE VIN
A Brera enoteca popular
with the fashion set.
Via San Marco, 2
Milan
+ 39 (0) 2 65 99650
WWW.NOMBRADEVIN.IT

DESIGN STORES

SPAZIO ROSANNA ORLANDI
Located in the posh Magenta
district, this boutique combines
furniture design and fashion.
Via Matteo Bandello, 14/16
Milan
+39 (0) 2 467 4471
WWW.ROSSANAORLANDI.COM

GALLERIA LUISA DELLE PIANE
Established in 1970 and opened to the
public in 1994, the gallery features
both contemporary art and furniture.
Via Giusti, 24
Milan
+39 (0) 2 29 06 17 72
WWW.GALLERIALUISADELLEPIANE.IT

THE ICONS

DOLCE&GABBANA

Italian tradition (black lace, Sicilian tailoring) meets sex appeal (leopard print and Madonna) in the signature collection of Domenico Dolce and Stefano Gabbana. Their youthful D&G line offers flashy takes on hot trends. **WWW.DOLCEGABBANA.COM**

FENDI

Fendi is pure Italian style interpreted by Karl Lagerfeld in gold, fur and gold-plated fur. On the clasp of the label's "It" bags (designed by Carla Fendi) its famous "double-F" logo is a symbol of the height of luxury. **WWW.FENDI.COM**

GIORGIO ARMANI

Armani is one of fashion's biggest empires, and the Giorgio Armani label is its pinnacle. Ultra-expensive and luxurious, its signatures are high-end suiting for men and women, and gowns favored by Hollywood's elite. **WWW.ARMANI.COM**

GUCCI

Gucci is Italian for glamour. Founded in 1921, the maison became a symbol of late '90s hedonism under American designer Tom Ford. Now under Frida Giannini, Gucci represents a subtler type of glamour, without losing a bit of its luxurious appeal. **WWW.GUCCI.COM**

MISSONI

Missoni's famous chevron print represents bohemian luxury at its finest. A family affair since 1953, the label is now run by Angela Missoni. **WWW.MISSONI.COM**

PRADA

Miuccia Prada is fashion's reigning sophisticate. Whether she's championing

GUCCI

GIORGIO ARMANI

warrior women or a return to femininity, Prada favors an intellectual statement to easy beauty. The younger Miu Miu line is a favorite of cool girls around the globe. **WWW.PRADA.COM**

VALENTINO

The designer known simply by his first name, and his signature shade of red dressed Jackie O. and Elizabeth Taylor and brought Roman verve to Milan. Current creative directors Pier Paolo Piccioli and Maria Grazia Chiuri keep his elegant vision evolving. **WWW.VALENTINO.COM**

VERSACE

Gianni Versace launched his eponymous label in 1978, and it became the place for high-glitz glamour. Since his 1997 murder, younger sister Donatella has continued the brand's storied—and sexy—legacy, herself the embodiment of the ultimate Versace girl. British designer Christopher Kane heads up second line Versus, inspired by the label's archive. **WWW.VERSACE.COM**

STORES

DOLCE&GABBANA
Via Della Spiga, 26
+39 (0) 2 760 011 55

FENDI
Via Sant'Andrea, 16
+39 (0) 2 760 216 17

GIORGIO ARMANI
Via Montenapoleone, 2
+39 (0) 2 760 032 34

GUCCI
Via Montenapoleone, 5-7
+39 (0) 2 771 271

MISSONI
Via Montenapoleone, 8
+39 (0) 2 760 035 55

PRADA
Corso Venezia, 3
+39 (0) 2 760 240 12

VERSACE
Via Montenapoleone, 11
+39 (0) 2 760 085 28

PRADA

VALENTINO

ALBERTA FERRETTI

Alberta Ferretti makes ultra-feminine dresses in draped layers of gauzy fabric. **WWW.ALBERTAFERRETTI.COM**

ALBINO

Albino D'Amato's French training is obvious in his voluminous draping and clean geometry. The look is feminine and slightly retro. **WWW.ALBINO-FENIZIA.COM**

BLUMARINE

Flirty, fun and sexy, Blumarine makes embellished dresses perfect for a getaway to Capri. **WWW.BLUMARINE.COM**

BOTTEGA VENETA

Famous for not flaunting its logo, the brand has become synonymous with understated, elegant luxury with a capital L since Tomas Maier brought it back into vogue. **WWW.BOTTEGAVENETA.COM**

DIESEL BLACK GOLD

Italy's famed denim label made the transition to ready-to-wear in 2009. Under Sophia Kokosalaki, the line features a high-end rocker vibe. **WWW.DIESEL.COM**

DSQUARED2

Canadian twins Dan and Dean Caten's DSquared2 is outrageously sexy—and campy. **WWW.DSQUARED2.COM**

EMILIO PUCCI

Peter Dundas brought Pucci's psychedelic swirls into the 21st century with rich hues and little party dresses that stay true to the house's heritage. **WWW.EMILIOPUCCI.COM**

ETRO

Veronica Etro heads the womenswear division of her father's label, famous for its paisley prints; cross-cultural inspiration and sumptuous high-end fabrics. **WWW.ETRO.IT**

GIANFRANCO FERRÉ

"Architectural" is the buzzword at Gianfranco Ferré. Interpreted by designersTommaso Aquilano and Roberto Rimondi it translates to powerful shapes and precise cuts. **WWW.GIANFRANCOFERRE.COM**

MARNI

Consuelo Castiglioni's quirky fashions for funky girls come in muted shades and artsy

BLUMARINE

DIESEL BLACK GOLD

DSQUARED2

retro prints, with geometric shapes echoed in the label's covetable jewelry. **WWW.MARNI.COM**

MOSCHINO
A little loud (in the best way possible), this superstar of the '90s has been rediscovered by young fashionistas. **WWW.MOSCHINO.COM**

NO. 21
Alessandro Dell'Acqua has returned with a new label and a sexy take on sophisticated sportswear.
WWW.NUMEROVENTUNO.COM

ROBERTO CAVALLI
The king of all things outrageous, Roberto Cavalli's sexy party dresses come with a lot of pizzaz—and leopard print.
WWW.ROBERTOCAVALLI.IT

SALVATORE FERRAGAMO
Italy's first name in footwear also creates clothing with a luxurious take on classic Italian sportswear
WWW.FERRAGAMO.COM

STORES

ALBERTA FERRETTI
Via Montenapoleone, 21/A
Milan
+39 (0) 2 760 030 95

BLUMARINE
Via Della Spiga, 42
+39 (0) 2 795 081

BOTTEGA VENETA
Via Montenapoleone, 5
Milan
+39 (0) 2 760 244 95

DIESEL
Corso di Porta Ticinese, 44
Milan
+39 (0) 2 894 209 16

DSQUARED2
Via Verri, 4
Milan
+39 (0) 2 896 916 99

EMILIO PUCCI
Via Montenapoleone, 14
Milan
+39 (0) 2 763 183 56

ETRO
Via Montenapoleone, 5
Milan
+39 (0) 2 760 050 49

GIANFRANCO FERRÉ
Via Sant'Andrea, 15
+39 (0) 2 780 406

MARNI
Via Della Spiga, 50
Milan
+39 (0) 2 763 17 327

MOSCHINO
Via Sant'Andrea, 12
Milan
+39 (0) 2 760 008 32

ROBERTO CAVALLI
Via Spiga, 42
Milan
+39 (0) 2 760 209 00

SALVATORE FERRAGAMO
Via Montenapoleone, 3
Milan
+39 (0) 2 760 000 34

ETRO

ROBERTO CAVALLI

SALVATORE FERRAGAMO

LONDON

1846 British designer Charles Frederick Worth,
"the father of haute couture," moves to Paris

1875 Department store Liberty & Co. opens on Regent Street

1912 Bespoke tailors Gieves & Hawkes move to No. 1 Saville Row

1960s Carnaby Street is the center of Swinging London fashion

1971 Vivienne Westwood and Malcolm McLaren open Let it Rock (later
called Sex), the King's Road boutique that created punk fashion

1980 Iconic magazine *The Face* launches in London

1983 The British Fashion Council forms to promote London as an international
fashion capital; organizes first major London Fashion Week

1984 John Galliano bursts on to the scene with his Central Saint
Martins graduation collection, "Les Incroyables"

1989 British Fashion Awards founded to celebrate British designers
and creatives; honorees have included model Kate Moss and
four-time Designer of the Year Alexander McQueen

1992 Topshop and Topman combine to form the world's largest
fashion store at the brand's Oxford Circus flagship

2010 London Fashion Week is the first of the "big four"
to broadcast fashion shows live online

LONDON: THE LOW LIFE OF HIGH FASHION

BY JEM GOULDING

London answers to no one, not least in style. The city is among the oldest standing fashion capitals, boasting a tradition of tailoring that dates back to the 1700s. Even the oh-so-French haute couture is a British invention, created by designer Charles Frederick Worth in the middle 19th century. As is the case with any super-established style power, the saturation of artistic endeavors in one hub can cloud a singular view of the city. The multitude of foreign creatives drawn to the city makes London style a hard thing to decipher.

One only has to stand and listen to the cigarette clusters of fashion students on the doorstep at Central Saint Martins to learn that a large number of London's design hopes-of-tomorrow hold English as their second language, and still others as their third. Though the most prestigious of art schools such as the Royal College of Art, Goldsmiths College and Central Saint Martins spawned British fashion designers Vivienne Westwood, John Galliano and the late Alexander McQueen, such nurturing institutions have

< (PREVIOUS SPREAD) LAURA FRASER AND ALICE DELLAL

made way for no end of international success on the British fashion market. London style is now less about where you are from, and more about where you went to school. The industry's contemporary champions include talented invaders such as the nouveau-iconic Richard Nicoll from Australia, the whimsical Erdem from Canada, the severely sexual German import Felder Felder, and king of street spangle Ashish from India. Even current talks-of-the-town Christopher Kane and J.W. Anderson are Scottish and

Irish, respectively. Interesting, if unconscious, colonial art-school backlash if ever there was one.

Unlike many hype towns like L.A. or Amsterdam, where masses of fickle hipsters swamp round the latest thing like bees, only to quickly move on to the next, London rarely forgets a trend, even the embarrassing ones. Walk around the city and you will see the surviving Teddy Boys and rocka- billy girls, the punks and goths, the dandies and the twee behavers, the Acid House ravers, the New Roman-

London will always have its die-hard music style clans; it's just a little more underground than before. The "dress code" has made a major comeback at many music nights around the city, and certain neighborhoods proudly retain their musical heritage. West is still home to the seminal reggae and blues carnival in Notting Hill; North London still incubates a blossoming British folk scene, boosting acts like Mumford & Sons, Mystery Jets and The Maccabees at venues such as The Flower Pot, The Old Queens Head and the late, great Nambucca; East London still rocks out the punks, the metal and more recently the American-inspired garage rock; whereas south of the river, it's hard to ignore the grime artists such as Dizzee Rascal and Giggs shaping the identity of U.K. hip-hop.

tic prancers, the reggae and ska dancers, and, of course, the mods. Each group peacocking around, segregated by their uniforms, yet each with the ability to melt into one another.

Through these varied identities, music and fashion meet to make art. Once it was easy to attach a sight to a sound and categorize these style subsets by which kind of venues they frequented and the music they bought. With the download revolution, young people no longer invest the same amount of money in music, and an element of loyalty to a scene has somewhat disintegrated. Still,

∧ CLOCKWISE FROM TOP RIGHT: TEA TIME AT AN ENGLISH DINER;
STREET SCENE; MODELS JEREMY YOUNG AND GEORGE BARNETT

CENTRAL SAINT MARTINS

Just as Goldsmiths College produced the Young British Artists of the 1990s, Central Saint Martins is the main exporter of young British designers today. At recent editions of London Fashion Week, up to half of the designers had passed through Saint Martins' doors.

Much of the famed art school's success is credited to Louise Wilson, the head of the competitive Master's Program in fashion, a program that has produced some of the most adventurous designers working today. Known for her sharp tongue and take-no-prisoners approach, she's helped to launch the careers of celebrated designers such as Christopher Kane, Louise Goldin and Gareth Pugh, not to mention the many students who go on to prestigious behind-the-scenes jobs with other labels.

At the end of the program, students' graduate collections are shown at London Fashion Week, a hot ticket for those seeking new talent. Alexander McQueen famously sold his entire CSM graduate collection to fashion icon Isabella Blow, while John Galliano's romantic 1984 BA collection, Les Incroyables, was quickly bought up by department store Browns.

For more on Central Saint Martins visit
WWW.CSM.ARTS.AC.UK

More recently, South London is perhaps responsible for another style comeback, as the legendary Stockwell Skatepark seems to be spilling skaters back out across London. It's an interesting resurgence of a movement, and a look, that had become something of endangered species. That is until the fixed-gear bikes clans began to multiply in numbers, congregating around the spots where skaters might have hung out before. This new concrete territorialism has not only formed a divide between the "fixies" and the skaters, but also a battle between the "hesh" versus "fresh" sense of style. ("Hesh" means not to care how you look, so in effect no one actually claims to be "hesh" because that would insinuate they care too much and thus not be "hesh.") Regardless, hesh is the dirty skinny jeans, the shrunken, beaten-up T-shirt, and the mesh cap. Fresh, is the opposite aesthetic, normally spotted on fixies: T-shirts sparkling clean and larger-fitting, verging on hip-hop sized, and slightly wide-fit jeans with a more '90s hip-hop vibe.

^ MUMFORD & SONS

LIBERTY OF LONDON

Since 1875, Liberty & Co. has been a London shopping icon. While it started out selling decorative objects, Liberty's famous Tudor-style store has become an international symbol of British style. Most famous of all are its signature Liberty prints—dainty florals and colorful animal and abstract patterns—that manage to be both classically conservative and totally subversive all at once.

Today the shop is also home to top British and international designers including exclusive items from Erdem, Michael Van Der Ham, Raquel Allegra and jewelry designer Eddie Borgo.

Liberty
Great Marlborough Street
Mayfair, London
+44 (0)20 7734 1234
WWW.LIBERTY.CO.UK

Machismo has returned to London style through the gang warfare in street sports, a true-blue caveman approach to fashion that was all but diluted for the last decade by the gay fashion mafia and flamboyant club night Boombox (R.I.P.).

Real menswear for men's men is back with a vengeance. The invasion of the perfectly imperfect boy models drew some much-need attention to men's fashion in London, which past the glory of Chris Bailey's upheaval at Burberry Prorsum, or the occasional Savile Row dinner, has felt monotonous in tone for well over decade. Who would have thought that London Fashion Week would ever have a men's day? It appears to be a keeper for the British Fashion Council, and with untold success so far it's an ever-increasing threat to the über-established men's fashion weeks in Paris and Milan. Now with London's newfound respect in menswear, the Continent may very well start to lose British designers, who instead of showcasing their collections away, will start to patriotically opt for the city that bred them. Consequentially, men's fashion is becoming more balanced again, now that new money is being pumped into an already promising business. Young starlets of London menswear such as Katie Eary and Christopher Shannon were hailed as the hope of tomorrow at their most recent

shows, which championed a young, fun and decidedly masculine look.

London is, now more than ever, a man's town. At times it seems that for every nice-looking boy, there are six nice-looking girls to vie for his attention, and of that small pool of handsome fellas, roughly 30 percent are gay. The result: London is a field day for the average male, and a poverty-stricken survival-of-the-fittest for the females. This interesting new reality in London has unsurprisingly had a

dramatic effect on women's style in London in two particular ways. Firstly, women, or at least the ones looking to pair up happily ever after with a "nice," take fewer fashion risks, opting for an aesthetic that's come to be known as "twee." Rather than shine in all the Technicolor flamboyance like the '90s acid ravers, '70s disco kids or psychedelic '60s sirens, twee ladies go the submissive, dream-wife route, so as not to intimidate potential suitors. Typically, the twee opt for traditional daytime activities. You'll

find them shopping for old books and hand-knitted cardigans on Camden Passage, Islington. Or pedaling their vintage bicycles along Regents Canal on their way to munch on cupcakes on London Fields, a patch of grass in Hackney, North East London,

populated in the summer months by a mix of twee, hungover pub dwellers, fashionistas, and fixed-gear bikers.

The second style bunch out to snag the city's handsome dudes are somewhat more provocatively dressed,

^ ELLIOT ATKINSON AUTUMN/WINTER 2010/2011 LOOKBOOK,
  SHOT IN ABNEY PARK CEMETERY IN STOKE NEWINGTON

yet altogether more conscious of the movement and trends on the catwalk.

In recent years, British womenswear has become so brazen and vampish, you'd be forgiven for thinking London has reverted back to the Restoration period, where prostitutes were as commonplace and respected as your baker or blacksmith. London ladies seem to do shorter, tighter and more transparent to quite a unique effect. Sleek and tactile fabrics such as fox fur, stretch suede and revealing open-knit wool are the order of the night for these fashionable filth-bags, normally teamed with a one-off, oversize leather jackets, ripped stockings, eight-inch Givenchy heels or something to the same frivolous effect, a heavily embellished designer handbag (starting in at a value of around £600) and oodles of solid gold and silver jewelry designed by none other than Dominic Jones (if she is lucky). The new London night vixen seems to get away with dressing like a cheap hooker but doing it with utter class.

The back-and-forth between street and catwalk shows no signs of slowing when it comes to this look, thanks to the femme fatale designs of Gemma Slack, who rarely strays from skintight black leather and steel bustiers; the cutaway shapes of Danielle Scutt; and new kid on

STYLE BUBBLE'S SUSANNA LAU >

REQUIRED READING
BLOGS

STYLE BUBBLE
Blogger Susanna Lau epitomizes the best of the blogosphere: quality writing, great photos and awe-inspiring personal style. **WWW.STYLEBUBBLE.CO.UK**

FACE HUNTER
Jet-setting street-style photographer Yvan Rodic captures the younger side of the style spectrum. In 2010, the photographer released his first book, featuring 300 photos from 30 countries. **WWW.FACEHUNTER.BLOGSPOT.COM**

PONYSTEP
Founded by Richard Mortimer, the man behind the once-legendary club night Boombox, Ponystep features fashion, music and art—plus top-notch parties—from a network of super-cool contributors. **WWW.PONYSTEP.COM**

INSIDE AM LUL'S CLOSET
Spanish-born Londoner Gala Gonzalez is an editorial favorite for her adventurous sense of style that combines classic pieces with a rock 'n' roll attitude. **WWW.AM-LUL.BLOGSPOT.COM**

THE STYLE SCOUT
Self-proclaimed "London's longest-running street fashion blog," the Style Scout provides wardrobe inspiration from Brick Lane and Portabello to Notting Hill. **WWW.STYLESCOUT.BLOGSPOT.COM**

REQUIRED READING
MAGAZINES

I-D Since 1980, *i-D* has featured the best in fashion from the runway and the streets, with a cheeky winking cover. **WWW.I-DMAGAZINE.COM**

DAZED & CONFUSED Established by editor Jefferson Hack and photographer Rankin, *Dazed & Confused* has offered the hottest fashion, film, music and more since 1992. **WWW.DAZEDDGITIAL.COM**

ANOTHER MAGAZINE This bi-annual glossy from the founders of *Dazed & Confused* offers a grown-up take on pop culture and politics. **WWW.ANOTHERMAG.COM**

THE INTERNATIONAL HERALD TRIBUNE The highbrow paper is home to critic Suzy Menkes, known for her no-holds-barred reviews and signature pompadour hairstyle. **WWW.GLOBAL.NYTIMES.COM**

LOVE After leaving *Pop* magazine superstylist Katie Grand launched *LOVE*, one of the decade's most anticipated magazines. **WWW.THELOVEMAGAZINE.CO.UK**

LULA Fashion gets a girly twist in this whimsical bi-annual magazine. **WWW.LULAMAG.COM**

BRITISH VOGUE The British edition of the world's most influential fashion magazine has featured Kate Moss on the cover over 25 times. **WWW.VOGUE.CO.UK**

TWIN This biannual fashion and art publication is more coffee table book than magazine. **WWW.TWINFACTORY.CO.UK**

EXIT It's all about world-class photography at this bi-annual fashion mag. **WWW.EXITMAGAZINE.CO.UK**

the block Elliot Atkinson, who mixed trailer-trash prints with skimpy Barbarella shapes to great accolade at his debut show.

Unlike other fashion capitals, such as Paris where the women live on cigarettes and bitching, or Milan where, despite what Fellini may have you believe, the average women is a mere A cup, London

^ JETHRO CAVE AND SOPHIE WILLING

designers seem to champion a buxom and curvaceous figure. The iconic cinched waistline brought to us by Westwood and McQueen in particular, with exaggerated hips and boobs, is still symbolic of a shape that is decadent, provocative and quintessentially London. Westwood more on the historical, regal silhouette, and McQueen a shape that screams futuristic sex-

bot over pirate wench—two styles that season upon season are ripped off by the high-street chains.

The British high street is like tabloid gossip: The guilty pleasure we all love to hate. Whereas before, high street chains were ripping of catwalk originals better than ever, now stores such as Topshop and H&M are getting the designers on board under the guise of "collaboration," a brutal reality of "if you can't beat 'em, join 'em," but nevertheless tempting of course. Most members of the public, on a half decent salary and with a half decent eye can sample the originality of designer clothing, or at least a happy medium. This middle-ground was pioneered by retail mogul Sir Philip Green, a man whose business savvy is so respected that his mere interest in the once-dwindling Marks & Spencer famously saved the retail chain from corporate buyout.

After the success of designer diffusion lines at the mammoth, one-stop shop, where young British designers sell their souls to the devil in return for mass exposure and financial reward, Green went a step further, inviting supermodel and British style icon Kate Moss to design her own line exclusive to Topshop. Contrary to prediction by the non-believers that the line would be a fad destined to flop after its first season, over two years and a dozen collections later, the Moss-Green collaboration still sells like hotcakes.

Sir Green was aware of how the British public can elevate their models to superstardom statue, a trait belonging to London like no other. Whereas New York and L.A. may obsess over film stars, London likes to hold some models in the

limelight instead. Young model Daisy Lowe's recent campaign for Louis Vuitton—joining icons Madonna and Scarlett Johansson, who previous posed for the brand—serves to demonstrate how we hold a unique-looking fashion model as every bit as important as a pop star or Hollywood screen siren.

Evidently, for some of the London model elite, it can sometimes be hard to determine where the movie stops and real life begins. No place does a trashy aristocrat model quite like London. One name that will echo for years to come is Alice Dellal, the property heiress, sister to celebrated shoe designer Charlotte Olympia, and goddaughter to Mick Jagger, and something of a London icon. If every "It" girl were like Alice, then "It" girl wouldn't be a term to cringe at.

Alice's provocative dress sense, punky haircuts, perpetually smudged eye make-up and taboo taste in men have set trends for urban fashion followers the world over, inspired by how she makes the otherwise cliché rebellious debutante look so damn cool. You only have to look around to see copycat attempts at Dellal's notorious half-shaved head, or the must-have combination of ripped fishnets, lace-up Dr. Martens boots and the minuscule leather biker jacket worn, fittingly, on morning-after struts.

DOVER STREET MARKET

Founded by designer Rei Kawakubo of Comme des Garçons, Dover Street Market is one of London's most cutting-edge shopping destinations.

Along with all 14 Comme des Garçons labels—including Junya Watanabe Comme des Garçons, Tao Comme des Garçons and CDG spinoffs Play Comme des Garçons and Comme des Garçons Tricot—the shop also features six floors of top international designers—from New York's Zero Maria Cornejo to Tokyo's Toga Archives and Parisian label Givenchy—all displayed side-by-side in a state of what Kawakubo has called "beautiful chaos."

Dover Street Market
17-18 Dover Street
Mayfair, London
+44 (0) 20 7518 0680
WWW.DOVERSTREETMARKET.COM

Dellal's attitude and style also began to gain major attention around the same time that the tattooed boy became the in-thing as far as the style council was concerned. London-based, tattooed and demigod-like supermodels like Ash Stymest and Josh Beech catapulted inked skin and mosh-pit charm to whole new levels in fashion, changing the face even of the luxury fashion houses along the way. Pinnacle fashion houses such as Hermès, Givenchy, Dior Homme and Gucci happily now have a punk-arse kid with tattoos and flesh tunnels front their catwalks and sometimes even their campaigns. Josh Beech, with his otherworldly beauty, infectious sense of humor and bedroom-floor fashion sense, is muse to Hedi Slimane, Mario Testino, Mert & Marcus and a whole host of influential fashion heads. He has become a mascot for not giving a fuck about fashion, but leading it at the same time.

A 21st-century embodiment of London style.

NEIGHBORHOODS

SHOREDITCH
Home to Spitalfields Market and Brick Lane, a haven for vintage clothing and antiques, this East London style hub houses many of London's coolest magazines, fashion PR agencies and art studios. It also has some of the best places to booze and pose.

SOHO
There's still nothing quite like the buzz of Central London's theaterland. By day an explosion of film, fashion and literary industries, by night a gay hotspot and home to some of the best restaurants in the country.

STOKE NEWINGTON
A more relaxed alternative Camden for vegan food and yoga, this North East neighborhood combines the Dalston fashion clan with Clissold Park hippies. It also claims the magnificent Abney Park Cemetery, a popular location for fashion shoots.

HAMPSTEAD
For classy rural village feel, frolic with a North London lover on the heath, following the footsteps of William Wordsworth and Jimi Hendrix.

WESTBOURNE PARK
The West London neighborhood is home to a modest spill-over of Notting Hill, a never ending line of one-off bars and restaurants and some of the quirkiest boutiques in London.

< VICTORIA PARK, EAST LONDON

HOTSPOTS

THE HAGGERSTON, DALSTON
A cool traditional pub with
blues nights by candlelight and
a renowned roast dinner.
438 Kingsland Road
Hackney, London
+44 (0) 20 7923 3206
WWW.MYSPACE.COM/THEHAGGERSTON

THE TATE MODERN, SOUTHWARK
A multi-story playground for the
artistically educated and curious
alike, close to the Lambeth skate
park and with the British Film
Institute just along the river.
53 Bankside
London
+44 (0) 20 7887 8888
WWW.TATE.ORG.UK

LONDON FIELDS, HACKNEY
During the summer months this
park is part amateur fashion
show, part grassy picnic ground,
part fixed gear bike circuit, part
morning after boozefest for
the hip Hackney hangover.

ICA (INSTITUTE OF CONTEMPORARY ARTS), WESTMINSTER
A stone's throw from Buckingham
Palace, the ICA is a gallery and cinema
space for those in the know. A key
live music venue in London, and one
of the best art-book shops around.
The Mall
London
+44 (0) 20 7930 3647
WWW.ICA.ORG.UK

PORTOBELLO ROAD, NOTTING HILL
An Aladdin's cave of antiques,
vintage clothing, books and
fine foods, all set in a chic and
historic West London scene.

< AN EVENT AT THE INSTITUTE OF
CONTEMPORARY ARTS

STYLE EXPERT
DANIELLE SCUTT

Danielle Scutt makes powerful clothing for women with attitude. Whether she's channeling Pop-y prints, Miami DayGlo, or putting a sexier spin on androgynous dressing, her designs make a statement all on their own.

HOW WOULD YOU DESCRIBE THE DANIELLE SCUTT LABEL?
Danielle Scutt is a womenswear label with a different design ethic; its strong recognizable identity brings together luxury and excellent innovative design. The juxtaposition of elegance with the harder edge of confidence and power appeals to the targeted clientele who are looking for more than a "dress to look pretty in." Danielle Scutt designs provide the wearer with a full and total look, deviating away from today's culture of mix and match fashion.

WHAT TYPE OF WOMAN DO YOU DESIGN FOR?
Strong and feminine.

WHERE IS COMPANY HEADQUARTERS?
Bethnal Green, London

IS NOW A GOOD TIME TO BE CREATIVE IN LONDON?
Yes, always.

∧ DANIELLE SCUTT AND DESIGNS FROM HER AUTUMN/WINTER 2010/2011 COLLECTION

HOW WOULD YOU DESCRIBE THE "LONDON LOOK?"
Youthful.

DOES THE CITY FIND ITS WAY INTO YOUR DESIGNS? HOW?
Yes, subconsciously.

YOU'RE PART OF A NEW WAVE OF YOUNG DESIGNERS—MANY FROM YOUR ALMA MATER, CENTRAL SAINT MARTINS—THAT'S REDEFINING LONDON FASHION. COULD YOU TALK ABOUT THAT?
It was a very inspiring time in my life.

WHERE DO YOU FIND INSPIRATION?
People.

IF YOU COULD LIVE IN ANY PLACE, ANY ERA, WHEN AND WHERE WOULD YOU CHOOSE?
Here and now.

ANY TIPS FOR STYLE SAVVY VISITORS TO LONDON?
Stay in the center, go to Buckingham Palace and pack a cagoule [raincoat].

For more on Danielle Scutt visit
WWW.DANIELLESCUTT.COM

MENSWEAR DESIGNER
CHRISTOPHER SHANNON

Christopher Shannon has always stood out from the crowd. After graduating from the prestigious Central Saint Martins, and stints with designer Kim Jones and top stylist Judy Blame, Shannon's talent was spotted by none other than Louise Wilson, the very woman who mentored Alexander McQueen. Shannon was awarded a scholarship, and he returned to St. Martins, earning an M.A. in menswear. He made his London Fashion Week debut to rave reviews in 2008 and ever since, his sophisticated take on streetwear— wearable, refined, masculine and never boring—has made him one of the most exciting figures in men's fashion.

HOW WOULD YOU DESCRIBE THE CHRISTOPHER SHANNON LABEL?

Ever evolving.

WHERE IS COMPANY HQ?

We have a really great studio space in North London. It's an old nail factory with a glass roof. Amazing in summer, awful in winter. It also has a great courtyard full of jasmine plants, which is perfect for sitting outside on sunny days.

WHAT TYPE OF MAN DO YOU DESIGN FOR?

I never know. I suppose I recognize the man I probably don't design for. Every season you see that different people buy the clothes. I think if the man was too defined I would get bored trying to predict his mood or needs.

HOW WOULD YOU DESCRIBE THE CURRENT STATE OF LONDON FASHION?

I don't massively involve myself. I obviously have loads of friends working in the industry so we share each other's woes. I think in terms of Fashion Week things are getting stronger again and also sponsors are finally thinking of ways to get designers into stores which is a massive improvement over London fashion just surviving on hype.

IS TODAY A GOOD TIME TO BE CREATIVE IN THE U.K.?

I think if you are a creative then you have to be no matter what the time. Its not like I would think, "Oh the credit crunch is tricky," and then go and get a job as a bus driver. That's not to say bus drivers don't have intensely creative personal time.

DOES THE CITY FIND ITS WAY INTO YOUR DESIGNS?

Yes, everyday. I'm so much more inspired by the people I see around than an afternoon doing pretentious photocopying at the British Library.

WHAT ABOUT YOUR NORTHERN ROOTS? DOES LIVERPOOL INFLUENCE THE CLOTHES YOU MAKE?

I think my background definitely defined my initial aesthetic. Liverpool has a very particular style and way of dressing. It's the home of the original casuals and also pretty much bore the WAGs "movement," [an over-the-top, sexy style made famous by the "wives and girlfriends" of high-profile soccer stars]. Also you develop your taste with the things you are exposed to.

OFTENTIMES WOMEN'S FASHION GETS ALL THE ATTENTION, WHILE THE GUYS TAKE A BACK-SEAT. COULD YOU TALK ABOUT THE CHALLENGES OF LAUNCHING A MENSWEAR LINE?

I think the main challenge in London is that all the buyers go to Paris. It's a really simple thing but makes such a difference. So it's getting to Paris in time but also holding something back for London Fashion Week. I think the challenges are similar for us all. Sometimes money makes it easier but that's no more valid than being hardworking or having a creative way of moving forward. You see designers with no cash do incredible

work and people who try and buy their
way forward really not get it together.

**IS IT A GOOD TIME FOR MENSWEAR IN
LONDON? HOW DOES IT COMPARE WITH
OTHER INTERNATIONAL CITIES?**
I don't know. I've only ever done it here.
That said, it's the only place where you
would get this platform. That can be quite
hardcore though, you do your show on
these tiny budgets scraping together favors
then you are judged in the press next
to the big houses, that's quite intense.

**CENTRAL SAINT MARTINS IS SUCH AN
IMPORTANT FORCE IN BRITISH DESIGN. WHAT
WERE THE MOST IMPORTANT THINGS YOU
TOOK AWAY FROM YOUR EXPERIENCE THERE?**
I did my B.A. there first and then went
into industry as an assistant and doing
pop styling. After a while I was unclear
about what I wanted to do so I went for
an interview for the M.A. I was really for-
tunate that Professor Louise Wilson liked
my work and gave me a scholarship. I
have mixed feelings about the B.A., when
I was there I just wanted to do the M.A.;
the work that Louise was doing with the
students was completely inspiring to me.
I think Saint Martins is a bit of a mixed
blessing, people who don't go there get to
be really bitter and that's not great when
you experience them. There's no doubt for
me it's the best; I wouldn't have wanted to
go anywhere else. I think the M.A. helped
me validate my point of view and that you
should always think about modernity rather
than self-indulgent masturbatory work.

**WHAT ESSENTIAL WARDROBE PIECES SHOULD
EVERY STYLISH LONDON LAD HAVE?**
Well probably his own identity and ideas.
Failing that you can't go wrong with
one of our anorak shirts from A/W10.

**ANY TIPS FOR STYLE-SAVVY
VISITORS TO LONDON?**
I went to see Grace Jones at the
Royal Albert Hall last night then for
dinner in Chinatown; those are the
nights that make London amazing
to be in. Make your own way.

For more on Christopher Shannon visit
WWW.CHRISTOPHERSHANNON.CO.UK

DESIGNER DIRECTORY

ICONS

ALEXANDER MCQUEEN

Alexander McQueen's meteoric rise is the stuff of fashion legend: From the East End to Savile Row to Saint Martins, McQueen became fashion's *enfant terrible*, then took his life at the top of his career. From his earliest collections, McQueen wowed with theatrical designs and equally theatrical presentations. He reinvented himself each season, but his hallmarks remained: history and hourglass shapes, extreme prints and patterns, birds, feathers and couture-level construction. The label will be continued by his longtime assistant Sarah Hughes.

4-5 Old Bond Street
Mayfair, London
+44 (0) 20 7355 0088
WWW.ALEXANDERMCQUEEN.COM

BURBERRY PRORSUM

Best known for its classic khaki trenchcoats and signature check pattern, British heritage brand Burberry got a new lease on life when designer Christopher Bailey took over in 2001. Bailey is credited with creating timely interpretations of label classics such as the trench, plus glamorous dresses in neutral hues and military-inspired pieces with a rock 'n' roll edge. For his work, Bailey was named Designer of the Year at the British Fashion Awards in 2005 and 2009, and Menswear Designer of the Year in 2007 and 2008.

21-23 New Bond Street
Mayfair, London
+44 (0) 20 7839 5222
WWW.BURBERRY.COM

ALEXANDER MCQUEEN

BURBERRY PRORSUM

PAUL SMITH

Paul Smith is the face of modern British tailoring, and rightfully so. He was the first designer to do "classic with a twist" and his colorful stripes and checks have been a fashion crowd favorite since he opened his first store in 1970. With no formal training, he launched a line, starting with shirts and focusing on quiality and traditional tailoring. By 1976 he made his Paris debut, and since then the label has expaned to include furniture and children's clothing. For contributions to fashion, Smith was knighted in 2000.

40-44 Floral Street
Covent Garden, London
+44 (0) 20 7379 7133
WWW.PAULSMITH.CO.UK

VIVIENNE WESTWOOD

Vivienne Westwood has been a fashion force since the 1970s, when she and Malcolm McLaren opened Let it Rock. The shop (later known as Sex, and still run by Westwood as World's End). is credited with creating the look of punk rock, a style frequently referenced in her work. Other recurring themes include pirates, bondage, the Victorian era and political messages. In addition to fashion, Westwood is known for her cheeky sense of humor, even recieving the Order of the British Empire *sans* knickers.

44 Conduit Street
Mayfair, London
+44 (0) 20 7287 3188
WWW.VIVIENNEWESTWOOD.COM

PAUL SMITH

VIVIENNE WESTWOOD GOLD LABEL

THE ESTABLISHMENT

GILES DEACON

Giles Deacon has sent Pac Man helmets and cartoon-cloud skirts down his runway. But it's his attention to detail—in addition to his irreverent style—that keeps him on top. In 2010, he was named creative director at Emanuel Ungaro, surely to bring a bit of fun to the venerable French house.

HUSSEIN CHALAYAN

Hussein Chalayan is best known for his robotic dresses and a wooden skirts. While always avant-garde, Chalayan is also a master of refined minimalism.
WWW.HUSSEINCHALAYAN.COM

JEAN-CHARLES DE CASTELBAJAC

Jean-Charles de Castelbajac creates fashionable riffs on pop culture.
WWW.JC-DE-CASTELBAJAC.COM

JONATHAN SAUNDERS

Color is at the core of Jonathan Saunders' designs, in patterned pastels or geometric blocks of saturated hues.
WWW.JONATHAN-SAUNDERS.COM

JULIEN MACDONALD

Welsh designer Julien Macdonald makes the world a brighter place with his bold party dresses that are not for the shy of heart. From 2001 to 2005 he was lead designer of Parisian label Givenchy.
WWW.JULIENMACDONALD.COM

MARIOS SCHWAB

Whether curve-hugging dresses or something more fluid, Marios Schwab's designs are always thoughtful and supremely feminine.
WWW.MARIOSSCHWAB.COM

HUSSEIN CHALAYAN

JONATHAN SAUNDERS

MATTHEW WILLIAMSON

Season after season, Matthew Williamson offers colorful feminine frocks with intricate details reminiscent of India and Ibiza.

WWW.MATTHEWWILLIAMSON.COM

SOPHIA KOKOSALAKI

Sophia Kokosalaki is known for chic and sexy clothing that nods to her Grecian heritage with lush draping and geometric details.

WWW.SOPHIAKOKOSALAKI.COM

STELLA MCCARTNEY

Stella McCartney made waves as the head designer of Parisian house Chloé, but it was when she launched her own label in 2001 that the world got to know her signature aesthetic. Always girly with a tomboy twist, McCartney is best known for her chunky knits and vegan-friendly designs. WWW.STELLAMCCARTNEY.COM

STORES

MATTHEW WILLIAMSON
28 Bruton Street
Mayfair, London
+44 (0)20 7629 6200

STELLA MCCARTNEY
30 Bruton Street
Mayfair, London
+44 (0) 20 7518 3100

MATTHEW WILLIAMSON

SOPHIA KOKOSALAKI

THE NEW GUARD

ASHISH

Indian-born designer Ashish Gupta has a way with embellishment: glitzy sequins, studs and embroidery on grungy, relaxed shapes. **WWW.ASHISH.CO.UK**

BASSO & BROOKE

The duo behind Basso & Brooke has chamionped wild digital prints and hi-tech finishes long before the look became the trend *du jour*.

WWW.BASSOANDBROOKE.COM

CHARLES ANASTASE

Born in France and based in London, Charles Anastase makes flirty, floaty clothing that girly girls love.

WWW.CHARLESANASTASE1979.COM

CHRISTOPHER KANE

Christopher Kane's tastefully tacky—and utterly covetable—clothing has referenced atomic bombs, Priscilla Presley and *Planet of the Apes*.

DANIELLE SCUTT

A trendsetter even among London's edgy catwalks, Danielle Scutt designs clothing that's always powerful, whether the season's look is '80s glam or subdued androgyny.

WWW.DANIELLESCUTT.COM

ERDEM

Ladylike yet youthful, Erdem's dainty dresses feature offbeat details such as 3-D florals and quirky colors. **WWW.ERDEM.CO.UK**

BASSO &BROOKE

ERDEM

GARETH PUGH

A true showman with a bent towards
the darker side of fashion, Gareth
Pugh quickly became a favorite of
critics—including Anna Wintour
herself—after graduating Central Saint
Martins. He now shows in Paris.

WWW.GARETHPUGH.NET

KINDER AGGUGINI

With an impressive resume including
stints on Savile Row, as well as at Galliano,
Vivienne Westwood and Versace, the
Italian-born former punk has quickly
built up a following for his signature
label after decades in the business.

WWW.AGGUGINI.COM

LOUISE GOLDIN

Louise Goldin first made her name
in knitwear, but short dresses with
exaggerated shapes and lots of sex
appeal have become her signature.

RICHARD NICOLL

Australian-born designer Richard Nicoll
creates supremely wearable, trend-setting
clothes for the modern working woman.
While other designers favor the formal,
Nicoll's talent lies in stylish daywear.

WWW.RICHARDNICOLL.COM

KINDER
AGGUGINI

RICHARD
NICOLL

THE UNDERGROUND

CHRISTOPHER SHANNON

Christopher Shannon challenges guys everywhere to step up their game with his thoughtful, fashion-forward streetwear.

WWW.CHRISTOPHERSHANNON.CO.UK

ELLIOT ATKINSON

Elliot Atkinson's sexy, sheer and cut-out frocks are totally on-trend with today's London look.

WWW.ELLIOTATKINSON.CO.UK

FELDER FELDER

Twin sisters Annette and Daniela Felder draw influence from their shared love of music, creating slim and sexy clothing for rock 'n' roll girls.

WWW.FELDERFELDER.COM

GEMMA SLACK

Gemma Slack slack creates clothing that's dark, sexy and totally modern, a style she honed as an apprentice to Gareth Pugh.

WWW.GEMMASLACK.COM

HOLLY FULTON

Art Deco is a recurring reference point for Holly Fulton's artfully ornamented, detail-oriented line.

WWW.HOLLYFULTON.COM

J.W. ANDERSON

Though only a few seasons in, J.W. Anderson's sophisticated menswear has such a strong following that he's branched into womenswear with a similar dark modernism. **WWW.J-W-ANDERSON.COM**

KATIE EARY

While many of London's menswear designers opt for sleek masculinity, Katie Eary offers up Technicolor prints and detailed fabrics usually reserved for womenswear. **WWW.KATIEEARY.COM**

FELDER
FELDER

HOLLY
FULTON

KRYSTOF
STROZYNA

KRYSTOF STROZYNA

Powerful, body-con shapes and sculptural jewelry are the signature looks of Polish-born designer Krystof Strozyna.
WWW.KRYSTOFSTROZYNA.COM

LOUISE GRAY

Louise Gray's training in textile design is evident in the her innovative use of color and texture—think bright pink fur and patterned patchwork.
WWW.LOUISEGRAYLONDON.COM

MARK FAST

Mark Fast may still be finding his footing, but sexy and shapely knitwear is his specialty. WWW.MARKFAST.NET

MEADHAM KIRCHHOFF

East Enders Ed Meadham and Benjamin Kirchhoff's dark, Victorian-inspired designs have made their's one of London's most exciting labels to watch.
WWW.MEADHAMKIRCHHOFF.COM

MARY KATRANTZOU

Over the seasons, Mary Katrantzou's digital prints have melted from rigid geometry to fluid swirls and back to recognizable forms, while her clothing has grown more structured.
WWW.MARYKATRANTZOU.COM

PETER PILOTTO

Designers Peter Pilotto and Christopher de Vos have made their mark on the London fashion scene with their bold use of color and prints on perfectly draped dresses.
WWW.PETERPILOTTO.COM

WILLIAM TEMPEST

This young designer offers a sophosticated and structured take on London's skin-tight trend. WWW.WILLIAMTEMPEST.COM

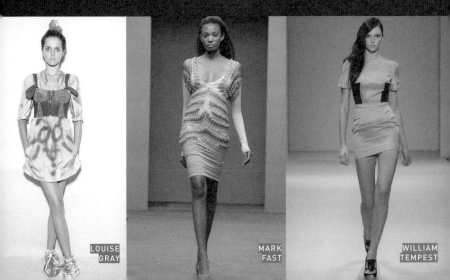

LOUISE GRAY

MARK FAST

WILLIAM TEMPEST

TOKYO

TOKYO:
THE STYLE SET

BY DAN BAILEY

Cities are often identified by their monuments and architecture, but Tokyo is constantly evolving and changing. Buildings disappear over night to be replaced by shining new earthquake-proof designs before you have chance to miss what was once there. A city that was destroyed twice in the last century has very little to preserve architecturally. This can be a developer's dream—unlike Paris or London, huge areas can be re-imagined, such as those at Roppongi Hills, Tokyo Midtown or Omotesando Hills. But what is the prevailing image of Tokyo? A *Blade Runner*-esque neon forest within a concrete jungle? Over the past decade, Tokyo has become as known for its street fashion as for anything else. And if there is a place that has become iconic in the visual vocabulary of what Tokyo is, it has to be Shibuya Crossing.

^ BABY MARY, MADEMOISELLE YULIA AND SNAPSHOTS FROM THE TOKYO CLUB SCENE
< (PREVIOUS SPREAD) A LOOK FROM SWAGGER SPRING/SUMMER 2010

The millions of people crossing the world's busiest pedestrian intersection everyday are impressive enough as a collective to warrant epic scenes in movies. But if you look closer, at the individuals, you see that Shibuya Crossing is where many of the subcultures in Tokyo cross paths. The *gyaru* girls with their tanned skin and bleached hair head up left towards shopping mall 109, a deafening beacon of kitsch *kawaii* (cute) style.

Older, wealthy shoppers change trains here to head out to the Ginza district with its gleaming high-fashion, high-price flagship stores, while the average shopper will head to the local department stores such as Parco, Seibu and Tokyu. Here, luxury boutiques within stores cater to the masses (it's said between 30 and 40 percent of all luxury goods

are sold within Japan; remember, Tokyo's well-known and influential street style represents just a fraction of the people living in the world's largest megalopolis.)

It's from Shibuya that the stylish people featured in magazines such as *FRUiTS* and *TUNE* or on street snap websites such as Drop Snap and Rid Snap head down to Harajuku.

In recent years, Harajuku has become well known for its tribes of Gothic Lolitas who gather in the space between Harajuku station and Yoyogi Park most Sundays. It's a different demographic that garners the attention of trend hunters and street fashion photographers, though. Running from the outside of the Laforet building and on towards Ralph Lauren and Omotesando Hills

is probably the world's greatest youth fashion runway. Anyone can get a front-row seat here on the railings that border the sidewalk, which, although wide by Tokyo standards, are always packed with people; the spot outside Lawson is prime for people-watching. If you hang around long enough, which I suggest you do, you will notice that some people will pass by a number of times, they are so keen to get snapped.

On Omotesando, known as the Champs-Élysées of Tokyo, the streets are ripe with the layered mix-and-match style of Japan's youth between luxury foreign labels such as Dolce&Gabbana, Ralph Lauren, Christian Dior and Chanel. Local labels as well as overseas brands are mixed with "used" and

"recycled" finds that are usually imported in bulk from America.

A lot of the layering and cuts take obvious style cues from the tradition of the Japanese avant-garde such as Comme des Garçons and Yohji Yamamoto, and as Style.com recently noted, some designers seem to have drawn inspiration from the streets here as well. The amazing thing is it never looks like people are trying too hard. Yes, a lot of thought has obviously gone into these outfits, but it just looks so "them" that it feels genuine and un-posed

As bold as some of the outfits may be, their wearers may actually be very shy. If a boy was to wear a skirt over leggings with a Mohawk and a ripped-up T-shirt on the streets of

London one would expect him to be rebellious in character. In Tokyo that's often not the case. The clothes do the talking on the street and in the clubs. (It can often be a case of style over substance; many times I have commented on a band T-shirt to be met with a blank look—the T-shirt was bought for how it looks, not who was on it.) In fact, most change into "room wear" as soon as they get back to their apartment. Their clothes are a stamp of identity, worn to face the world.

Freedom to dress in such a unique manner can be curtailed by the need to enter "grown-up" society; such is the strength of the social systems that operate in Japan. When they graduate from University among the cherry blossoms at the end of

REQUIRED READING

FRUITS/ TUNE / STREET
The granddaddy of street snap magazines, *FRUiTS* captures the cool kids of Harajuku. Sister publication *Tune* focuses strictly on the boys while *Street* imports inspirational looks from New York and beyond. **WWW.STREET-MG.COM**

COMMONS&SENSE
High-end bilingual magazine *Commons&Sense* features cutting-edge fashion from around the world distilled through editor Kaoru Sasaki's point of view. **WWW.COMMONS-SENSE.NET**

GOTHIC & LOLITA BIBLE
An offshoot of street-snap mag *Kera*, the *Gothic & Lolita Bible* is the essential authority on all things *visual-kei*. The seasonal publication—half magazine, half book—is available in the U.S. through Tokyopop. **WWW.TOKYOPOP.COM**

VOGUE NIPPON
The Japanese edition of *Vogue* is home to tastemaker extraordinaire and street-style photog favorite Anna Dello Russo. **WWW.VOGUE.CO.JP**

VIVI
While hardly cutting-edge, this popular magazine for girls approaches fashion with an independent, empowered message. **WWW.NETVIVI.CC**

BOOKS
Stylist and fashion journalist Tiffany Godoy has lived in Tokyo since 1997, and has published two of the most definitive tomes on Tokyo fashion:2007's *Style Deficit Disorder*—a guide to Harajuku street fashion—and the 2009 follow-up *Japanese Goth*, which explores the unlikely combination of macabre and cuteness in Tokyo's Gothic Lolita subcultures.

March, young graduates go straight to work at the start of April. In this way, the famous springtime blossoming of cherry trees throughout Japan serves as a metaphor for the fleeting nature of youth.

From latest trends one week to suits and uniforms the next, the majority join the armies of salary men and office ladies working from eight in the morning until the last train at around 11 at night. They will have little time for their old haunts. Time with friends will be substituted for time with colleagues, 99 percent of the time this means an *izakaya* pub—not a bar or club. It is likely that anyone you meet at a club over the age of 22 has made a lifestyle or career choice that gives them the opportunity to wear what they want to work and still be able to define themselves with their own unique style. Often this means working as shop staff for the brands they like.

It's the people who work in these stores and their friends that populate the club nights you see on blogs such as Tokyodandy.com and at places including Trump Room and Trump House, EVER, Chelsea Hotel, La Fabrique and at the exclusive Le Baron in Aoyama. It is a closely knit circle that includes all types of Tokyo fashion insiders. They are the "kids" who work at hair salons such as Shima,

BLOGS

TOKYO DANDY
The dashing duo of Dan Bailey and Kazuaki Joe K present bi-lingual coverage of Tokyo fashion from the runway to the street, with everything from Harajuku parties to high-fashion events.
WWW.TOKYODANDY.COM

DROP
Daisuke Yokota snaps Tokyo's most stylish citizens for a regular dose of creative, colorful and sometimes downright freaky fashion. **WWW.DROPSNAP.JP**

STYLE FROM TOKYO
Former *FRUiTS* photog Reo Shito takes her trusty Canon camera to the streets to capture the real-life styles around Harajuku and other fashionable hoods. **WWW.REISHITO.COM**

FASHIONSNAP/STREET SNAP
News and trends straight from Tokyo, plus daily street-style sightings. Bi-lingual, though the English site is in need of an update. **WWW.FASHIONSNAP.COM**

TOKYO FASHION
News, shopping guides and street snaps—English-language online magazine Tokyo Fashion is a one-stop shop for Tokyo style, whether your look is Gothloli, Fairy Kei or a little less extreme. **WWW.TOKYOFASHION.COM**

STYLE ARENA
Administered by the Japan Fashion Association, this site features interviews, street snaps and a shopping guide updated every Wednesday, plus a handy guide to the city's fashion tribes.
WWW.STYLE-ARENA.JP/EN

LAFORET

Harajuku landmark Laforet opened in 1978, and since then it's become home to some of the city's coolest fashions—and its best people-watching.
The seven-story mall is dedicated exclusively to edgy and youthful labels, including all the expected Harajuku Goth and Lolita looks that appeal to the local teen scene.

For the more sophisticated shopper, Laforet also offers British import Topshop as well as emerging local labels. In fact, the mall is the place where some of Harajuku's biggest exports got their start, including Hysteric Glamour.

WWW.LAFORET.NE.JP

which has salons throughout the city. Shima's Creative Director, Yuya Nara, works out of the Harajuku branch and has become something of a style icon himself. Professionally, he has recently taken care of Lady Gaga and the Olsen sisters when they have visited Tokyo.

Like much of the style set, Nara and his team from Shima will often pick up clothes from Faline's Toyko store, owned by another Harajuku icon, Baby Mary. She is an unofficial ambassador of Tokyo fashion; when not at her Harajuku store or one of her two stores in Nagoya she will be partying with close friend Jeremy Scott at Coachella or overseas at

one of the international fashion weeks. At Faline, Scott's clothes hang beside clothing by another of Mary-san's friends, Marjan Pejoski, who became the first foreign designer at a Japanese label when he took over at Dress Camp.

The girls who work at Faline are party regulars and their friend, Mademoiselle Yulia, will often be caught here picking up outfits from Faline's pink and patterned filled racks for her growing number of international club appearances. A DJ and MC with trademark blue hair, Yulia has seen her star rapidly rise over the past couple of years. Her second mix-album was released in 2009 and her own jewelry label GIZA is stocked in the areas best boutiques, including Phenomenon, the shop owned by designer Big-O, another Tokyo icon with musical roots. Big-O is old school Japanese hip-hop and Phenomenon is fast becoming the go-to store for Japanese boys. The brand is evolving gradually from a well-dressed b-boy look to a more eclectic streetwear style of late, including out-there looks like fringed leather vests and paisley-printed harem pants.

Back towards Shibuya, the iconic boutique Milkboy is the home base of club favorite DJ 2Boy, who mixes everything from Detroit techno to

dub reggae and Japanese pop. He has made Milkboy's trademark patterned suits his signature, whether in his frequent appearances in best-selling hairstyle magazine *choki choki* or playing events, where he will often be on the bill alongside the DJ unit SEX. Takeshi and E. miko are the duo behind SEX, and they're also the designers behind the new label DRESSEDUNDRESSED. The label's flowing black clothing is the epitome of subtle Tokyo goth-mode style. Such is the nature of Tokyo's tight-knit style network.

Further back towards Shibuya is the Sister store, run by some of the

best-dressed girls in the city. In the same building as Sister, Candy mixes well-selected vintage with a slew of edgy brands from both Japan and overseas. Candy has been an iconic store for a generation of Harajuku kids, and it's a prime example of how fashion and art are slowly beginning to collaborate at a grassroots level—the space often hosts exhibitions from new and upcoming artists. Stores and labels like this are defining the scene all over Tokyo.

Meanwhile, international fast-fashion stores including H&M and Forever 21 have recently opened in Shibuya and Harajukju, as they already have in

^ PHENOMENON'S HARUJUKU FLAGSHIP

Ginza. Yet on the streets of Tokyo you very rarely, if ever, see people wearing the same outfit. Especially in Harajuku, where you will see the same kind of look, but never made up from the same items of clothing. If people wear a stamp of identity, they don't want to be the same as anyone else.

With this encroaching of fast-fashion some are seeing a move out to more suburban areas such as Koenji, which has great restaurants, used stores and a growing number of independent shops such as those in the Kitakore building.

Tokyo's street fashion will continue to grow and evolve as quickly as the buildings and streets within which Tokyoites live, eat and shop. The reverence for Western culture once attributed to the Japanese is being replaced by a more self-confident attitude. These kids have seen themselves in international magazines such as *i-D* and *Dazed & Confused*. They know their Asian neighbors look up to their style.

As Japanese companies generate headlines for their technological developments the more fashion-conscious amongst us wonder: Where will the Japanese style pioneers take us next?

EXTREME STYLE

Two main looks dominate foreign perceptions of Japanese fashion. The first is the dark and intellectual design pioneered by the likes of Yohji Yamamoto and Rei Kawakubo of Comme des Garçons. The other is the exact opposite: the over-the-top, often costume-y fashion of Harajuku's teen scene. But with so many subcultures—and subdivisions of those—how do you know if you're looking at a Loligoth or a Ganguro? Here's a handy guide.

GANGURO
The look: Tokyo's "black face girls" sport dark tans with white lipstick and eye makeup, and extreme bleach-blonde hair

Spot them: At Shibuya's tanning salons

GYARU
The look: Less extreme than the ganguro, Japan's version of the California girl sports short shorts, high heels and a deep tan

Spot them: Shopping for the latest looks at Shibuya 109

LOLITAS
The look: Lolitas, and their darker counterparts, the Gothic Lolitas, wear sweet and girly Victorian-inspired dresses with an air of innocence

Spot them: Stocking up on frilly frocks at Harajuku hangouts Baby the Stars Shine Bright, Metamorphose and h.NAOTO.

ROCKABILLY
The look: A throwback to old-fashion American rock 'n' roll, the bad boys of the Tokyo Rockabilly Club wear lots of leather and slicked-back hair

Spot them: Doing the twist in Yoyogi Park

A BATHING APE

Around the world, streetwear is tied to hip-hop and skate culture. In Tokyo it's tied, above all, to Nigo.

The man behind A Bathing Ape, Nigo, was born Tomoaki Nagao; his nickname (meaning "second version") is a nod to Hiroshi Fujiwara, the influential DJ and tastemaker considered the godfather of Harajuku style. But while Fujiwara opted to stay behind the scenes, quietly putting out products without his name attached, Nigo made his name with his brand's limited-edition T-shirts and covetable, collectable sneakers, plus high-profile collaborations with the likes of Pharrell Williams of the Neptunes and, more recently, Kanye West. Since its 1993 inception, all Bape products are released in limited qualities at only a few select stores—it's not unusual to see long lines camped overnight outside a store when a new product is released, or sky-high resale prices among collectors.

Bapexclusive Aoyama
5-5-8 Minami-Aoyama
Minato-ku, Tokyo
+81 (0) 3 3407 2145
WWW.BAPE.COM

TOKYO'S CLUB SCENE >

NEIGHBORHOODS

AOYAMA / OMOTESANDO
Tokyo's high-end shopping mecca is home to the landmark Comme des Garçons flagship, as well as the upscale Omotesando Hills mall and hip boutique Loveless. Shopping here is pricey and all about designers.

GINZA
Filled with tourists and traffic, Ginza is a must-see shopping destination that features the most luxurious of the international luxury brands, like Chanel, Louis Vuitton and Gucci, plus the unlikely new addition of a 12-story Abercrombie & Fitch.

SHIBUYA
The ultimate shopping destination for the young and hip, Shibuya features Tokyo's most exciting new boutiques, plus the massive shopping mall Shibuya 109, which serves up loud looks to a slightly younger crowd.

HARAJUKU
For many, Harajuku is the international face of Tokyo fashion, the place where young people out-dress each other for a chance to be noticed by street snap photographs on the main drag, Meiji Dori, while hip shops populate the serpentine backstreets of Ura-Hara.

NAKAMEGURO
Away from the crowds, under-the-radar neighborhood Nakameguro is becoming as Tokyo's capital of refined cool thanks to shops like the cult favorite Cow Books.

< BEDROCK BOUTIQUE, OMOTESANDO HILLS

TRUMP ROOM

As glamorous as it is exclusive, Trump Room is filled with fashionistas dancing among a lush interior of mirrors and chandeliers to the latest live bands and DJs.
Hoshi Building 4F, Jinnan 1-12-14
Shibuya-ku, Tokyo
+ 81 (0) 3 3770 2325

TRUMP HOUSE

The sister club to Trump Room, Trump House features the same outsize opulence, with high end-cocktails served in a rococo setting.
Hagi Building B1F, 2F 1-6-5 Dogenzaka
Shibuya-ku, Tokyo
+81 (0) 3 6809 0850

LE BARON DE PARIS

This sophisticated Aoyama club—an offshoot of the Paris venue of the same name—is as exclusive as it gets. Want even more privacy? Slip into the V.I.P. room, which features private karaoke, if you can make it past the velvet rope.
Aoyama Center Building, B1
3-8-40 Minami-Aoyama
Minato-ku, Tokyo
+81 (0) 3 3479 1766
WWW.LEBARON.JP

CHELSEA HOTEL

A grungy little rock club with graffiti-covered walls.
4-7-B1, Udagawa-cho
Shibuya-ku, Tokyo
+81 (0) 3 3770 1567
WWW.CHELSEAHOTEL.JP

< TRUMP ROOM

STYLE EXPERT

BABY MARY

Faline Tokyo is one of Harajuku's hot-test shops. The teeny-tiny, hot-pink shop boasts an impressive line-up of labels—including Jeremy Scott and Marjan Pejoski. But that's not its only claim to fashion cred. Faline is also the homebase of shop owner Baby Mary, a Tokyo style icon and member of the international jet set. Turns out, she's just a fun as the clothes she stocks.

HOW WOULD YOU DESCRIBE FALINE TOKYO?

Faline is like Baby Mary's room!! Dress for party! Ts & denim for the street! Lovely clothes for boy meeTs girl♥!!

Tea for afternoon, champagne for cocktail ...sexy lingerie for in bed, bikini for holiday, for boyz & girls!!! Fall in love !! Fun! Fun! Fun!!

WHAT LABELS DO YOU STOCK?

Jeremy Scott, KTZ, Fifi Chachnil, Ksubi, Corto Moltedo, Cassette Playa ... etc., etc.

WHAT DESIGNERS ARE YOU MOST EXCITED ABOUT RIGHT NOW?

Maison Michel, Charlotte Olympia.

∧ BABY MARY AND HER HARAJUKU BOUTIQUE FALINE TOKYO

ARE THERE JAPANESE DESIGNERS YOU WISH MORE PEOPLE KNEW ABOUT?
Phenomenon.

WHAT TYPE OF CUSTOMERS SHOP HERE?
We called them "Faline kids" they are soooo cute! Pop! Edgy! Tokyo new fashionista!!

HOW WOULD YOU DESCRIBE HARAJUKU?
Harajuku has everything!!!!! People don't care what to wear!! Freedom, dream, full of color!! Exciting but also relaxing. It's like an Asian N.Y.C. bit more calm♥!

It is Harajuku!!! Harajuku kids are gorgeous! Fabulous! Glamorous!!!

DO YOU HAVE ANY TIPS FOR STYLISH PEOPLE VISITING TOKYO? WHERE TO GO?
Meiji Jingu [shrine] for power spot!! Tabloid, a new trendy spot!

WHAT TO DO?
Onsen [hot springs]!! Do something Japanese-ie!!! Brown Rice Cafe for vegetarian! Or shopping @ Harajuku! Or whatever romantic♥ visit for cherry blossoms season!! It's beautiful!!!!!

WHAT TO WEAR?
What to wear?? Come to Faline Tokyo!

Faline Tokyo
1-7-5 Jingumae
Shibuya-ku, Tokyo
+81 (0)3 3403 8050
For more on Faline visit
WWW.BAMBIFALINE.COM

STREET SCENE
DROP SNAP

The streets around Harajuku station are filled with people dressed to the nines, hoping to catch the eye of a photographer for the so-called street snaps that show up in various magazines and websites. While the U.S. and Europe have only recently caught on to the street style trend, in Japan it's these everyday people, not the models in magazines, who inspire trends. One of the most popular sites is Daisuke Yokota's Drop Snap, which offers a daily does of what Tokyo's coolest residents are wearing.

HOW WOULD YOU DESCRIBE DROP?
DROPは東京のリアルでクールなストリートスナップを毎日配信している、今世界からも注目されている東京ストリートウェブマガジンです。個人的な趣味で2007年からDROPは始まりました。

Drop is a web magazine that publishes on-the-ground cool street fashion in Tokyo on a daily basis. We have a global following but it started in 2007 as a personal hobby.

HOW WOULD YOU DESCRIBE TOKYO STYLE TO-DAY? DOES ONE "TOKYO STYLE" EVEN EXIST?
いわゆる90年代に良く言われていた、デコラ系やビジュアル系などの奇妙なファッションから、コレクションなどから影

^ HARAJUKU FASHIONS FROM DROPSNAP.JP

響を受けたシックでクールなストリート
スタイルが定着しつつあります。しかし
そこには日本人なりの遊び心を持った
ファッションもうまく共存しています。

There's a lot of sick, cool street fashion
that's been influenced by fashion collections and weird movements like
the so-called *decora-kei* and *visual-
kei* movements of the '90s, but the
Japanese spirit of playfulness always
coexisted with those fashions.

WHAT IS THE CORE OF TOKYO STYLE?

東京の中心で影響力を持つファッションア
イコン達の存在です。彼らがストリートのト
レンド牽引しています。Drop blogs に参
加している人はまさにそういう存在です。

It is the existence of fashion icons who have
real influence at the center of Tokyo. They
make street trends happen. The people who
contribute to Drop are just such people.

WHAT ARE THE BIGGEST INFLUENCES ON TOKYO STREET FASHION?

2000年代は間違いなく、エレクトロミュ
ージックとリンクしたアンダーグラウンド
のパーティーシーンでした。2010年はま
だ何が影響を及ぼすか分かりません。

The 2000s were without a doubt most
influenced by the underground party
scene associated with electronic music.
It's too early to tell what's going to
influence us in the next decade.

AFTER PHOTOGRAPHING SO MANY STYLISH PEOPLE, HAVE YOU LEARNED ANY STYLE TIPS?

はい。バランス感覚が上手いと、スト
リートではヒーローになれます。

Yes. If you're good at balance you
can be a street fashion hero.

For more visit **WWW.DROPSNAP.JP**

STYLE EXPERT
TOGA

Yasuko Furuta of the Tokyo-based label TOGA creates crisply tailored garments that have little to do with the flowing robes of ancient gods and beer-soaked frat parties that share her label's name. Instead she creates intellectual clothing for customers with what she describes as a "feminine and complex mentality."

With references as far-ranging as architecture, the Wild West and British Teddy Boys, the line combines "past, now, future, avant-garde, mixed elements of sense" with a "sense of exaltation," she says. TOGA also combines traditional Japanese dress with Western influences, and the deconstructed, avant-garde sensibilities of Comme des Garçons. However, the designer is quick to say she doesn't start with nostalgia, or a particular market in mind. In fact, her inspirations come together as the designs progress: "It is not inspired from a one clear phenomenon, but the design is always constructed by many images and phenomena in daily life. As a result,

it gradually becomes clear as a definite keyword at the production process."

Before launching her line in 1997, Furuta studied fashion at Paris's venerable Esmod fashion institute and worked as a stylist and costume designer—which helps explain why her delicately layered looks are so divinely wearable. Her attention to detail and lush fabrics won the attention of the Swiss Textile Federation, who nominated her for an award in 2008 along with the likes of Rodarte and Louise Goldin.

In addition to three TOGA boutiques in Japan, the line is available at select stores around the globe, including London's Dover Street Market.

For more on Toga visit **WWW.TOGA.JP.**

^ DESIGNER YASUKO FURUTA AND LOOKS FROM TOGA'S
SPRING/SUMMER 2010 TRANS ROMANTICS COLLECTION

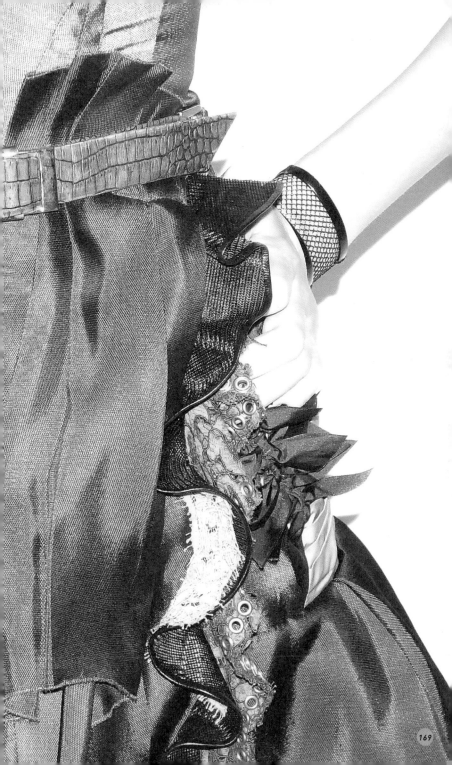

THE ESTABLISHMENT

ISSEY MIYAKE

One of the founding fathers of contemporary Japanese fashion, ISSEY MIYAKE creates imaginative and innovate clothing that combine artistry and technology. Plenty of secondary lines—like the charming PLEATS PLEASE ISSEY MIYAKE—keep customers happy. **WWW.ISSEYMIYAKE.COM**

COMME DES GARÇONS

Minimalist, sculptural and always on the cutting edge, the label founded by Rei Kawakubo is mysterious as the notoriously enigmatic designer herself. The line has expanded to include more than a dozen labels including Tao COMME des GARÇONS by Tao Kurihara and Junya Watanabe's signature line.

NEXT WAVE

JUNYA WATANABE

Rei Kawakubo's one-time protégé is known for his sharp tailoring and innovative use of fabric, cutting and draping. Still a part of COMME des GARÇONS, Watanabe's signature label is available at COMME des GARÇONS boutiques.

JUN TAKAHASHI UNDERCOVER

Jun Takahashi's boundary-pushing garments feature high-tech, utilitarian materials backed by extensive research and development—the designer even counts Rei Kawakubo as a fan. **BLOG.HONEYEE.COM/JTAKAHASHI**

ISSEY MIYAKE

COMME DES GARÇONS

YOHJI YAMAMOTO

Since the early 1980s, Yohji Yamamoto's avant-garde, anti-trend (and often black or white) garments have been synonymous with Tokyo fashion. His intellectual designs are always expertly executed, and always among fashion's most original.
WWW.YOHJIYAMAMOTO.CO.JP

LIMI FEU

Following in the steps of her famous father, Limi Yamamoto launched her own line in 2000, making wearable clothes with a younger, more rock 'n' roll aesthetic, and showing her collections in Paris. **LIMIFEU.COM**

STORES

ISSEY MIYAKE / AOYAMA
3-18-11 Minami-Aoyama
Minato-ku, Tokyo
+81 (0) 3 3423 1408

COMME DES GARÇONS AOYAMA
5-2-1 Minami-Aoyama
Minato-ku, Tokyo
+81 (0) 3 3406 3951

YOHJI YAMAMOTO AOYAMA
5-3-6 Minami-Aoyama
Minato-ku, Tokyo
+81 (0) 3 3409 6006

JUN TAKAHASHI UNDERCOVER
UNIMAT Bleu Cinq Point #A 1 F/B1F
5-3-22 Minami Aoyama
Minato-ku, Tokyo
+81 (0) 3 3407 1232

LIMI FEU HARAJUKU
Villa Hase 1F 6-6-11 Jingumae
Shibuya-ku, Tokyo
+ 81 (0) 3 5464 1752

YOHJI YAMAMOTO

LIMI FEU

SHOPPING GUIDE

A BATHING APE

A streetwear label with a cult-like following, A Bathing Ape is the home of limited-edition everything: shoes, caps and custom cut-and-sewn tees and hoodies. **WWW.BAPE.COM**

BEDROCK

It's all a bit mysterious, but for those in the know, Maniac Corporation is the mastermind behind some of Tokyo's best clothes—even getting to their "secret" subterranean boutique takes some detective work. Shoppers must first descend a spiral staircase hidden in the Forbidden Fruit café in the Omotesando Hills mall, to get to an underground lair filled with dark designs from the likes of Rick Owens, Givenchy and Maniac's own L.G.B. and IF SIX WAS NINE. **WWW.MANIAC-CO.JP**

CANDY

Select shop Candy features a mix of vintage and new designs from the likes of Mikio Sakabe. **WWW.CANDY-NIPPON.COM**

DRESS CAMP

A perennial favorite at the Tokyo Collections, Dress Camp brings the best of fashion history together with innovative materials and a thoroughly modern attitude—recent designs referenced the Orient Express and the work of Fritz Lang. Now that boundary-pushing Macedonian designer Marjan Pejoski has taken over, the label is hotter than ever. **DRESSCAMP.JP**

FALINE TOKYO

Helmed by Tokyo party girl Baby Mary this teeny hot-pink Harujuku boutique features playful looks for the likes of streetwear giants from the U.S. and Japan, including Alife, Vans, Dim Mak Collection, RVCA and British label KTZ. **BAMBIFALINE.COM**

FUR FUR

Feminine and fun, Aya Furuhashi's Fur Fur label mixes flowing, ladylike dresses, structured jackets and distressed pieces, available online and at the brand's Laforet shop. **WWW.FURFURFASHION.COM**

CANDY

L.G.B.

FUR FUR

STORES

GALAXXXY
Bold prints meet neon at this Shibuya shop, which features its own DJ, art exhibitions and a seriously '80s vibe.
WWW.JOE-INTER.CO.JP

G.V.G.V.
G.V.G.V. is a sophisticated line of strong, body-conscious looks with a feminine edge from designer Mug. **WWW.GVGV.JP**

GRIMOIRE
Grimoire stocks romantic vintage garments and accessories in a shop with a mystical European vibe. **WWW.GRIMOIRE.JP**

HYSTERIC GLAMOUR
Filled with tongue-in-cheek riffs on American rock 'n' roll culture from the '60s, '70s and '80s—and with a little sex mixed in for good measure—Hysteric Glamour has been a favorite since 1983. **HYSTERICGLAMOUR.US**

A BATHING APE
Bapexclusive Aoyama
5-5-8 Minami-Aoyama
Minato-ku, Tokyo
+81 (0) 3 3407 2145

BEDROCK
West Building B1F
Omotesando Hills
4-12-10 Jingumae
Shibuya-ku, Tokyo
+81 (0) 3 3423 6969

CANDY
1F FAKE 18-4
Udagawa-cho
Shinjuku-ku, Tokyo
+81 (0) 3 5456 9891

DRESS CAMP
5-5-1 Minami-Aoyama
Minato-ku, Tokyo
+81 (0) 3 5778 3717

FALINE TOKYO
1-7-5 Jingumae
Shibuya-ku, Tokyo
+81 (0) 3 3403 8050

FUR FUR
Laforet Harajuku 2F,
1-11-6 Jingumae
Shibuya-ku, Tokyo
+81 (0) 3 3770 3084

GALAXXXY
Shibuya Land Bldg 1F
2-23-10 Dogenzaka
Shibuya-ku, Tokyo
+81 (0) 3 3461 2033

G.V.G.V.
8F Shinjuku
Takashimaya 5-24-2 Sendagaya
Shibuya-ku, Tokyo
+81 (0) 3 5361 1074

GRIMOIRE
7F Terusu Jinnan
1-10-7 Jinnan
Shibuya-ku, Tokyo
+81 (0) 3 3780 6203

HYSTERIC GLAMOUR
6-23-2 Jingumae
Shibuya-ku, Tokyo
+81 (0) 3 3409 7227

G.V.G.V.

DRESS CAMP

GRIMOIRE

SHOPPING GUIDE

LIFT

An upscale boutique featuring the likes of Damir Doma and Label Under Construction—Lift prides itself on going beyond the usual retail experience, to teach and inspire shoppers.
WWW.LIFT-NET.CO.JP

MILK

A Harajuku landmark, Milk is the place where Lolita style was born, and for over 30 years the shop has been selling sweet and girly retro-style duds. Next door, Milkboy offers up graphic streetwear and limited-edition sneaker collabos for the boys.
WWW.MILK-WEB.NET

MISTER HOLLYWOOD

Daisuke Obana's too-cool store features his own line of architectural, vintage-inspired menswear N. Hoolywood as well as tons of retro Americana kitsch imported from frequent research trips to LA.
WWW.N-HOOLYWOOD.COM

PHENOMENON

Phenomenon combines the best of hip-hop and rock 'n' roll, with nods to old-school New York and traditional Japanese craftsmanship, for out-there looks that still stay wearable.
WWW.PHENOMENON.TV

SISTER

Vintage shop Sister is the place where Tokyo's coolest girls go for fashion-forward retro looks, along with edgy accessories by select emerging designers, like lacy underthings from Yes Master and edgy jewelry by Erickson Beamon. **WWW.SISTER-TOKYO.COM**

SWAGGER

Swagger is the brainchild of rapper Big-O and Ignition Man. Established in 1999, Swagger's smart streetwear is hotter than ever thanks, in part, to collaborations with top artitsts from around the world.
WWW.SWAGGER-CO.COM

MISTER HOLLYWOOD

MILK

SISTER

STORES

TOGA
Designer Yasuko Furuta creates playful and feminine clothes that are supremely wearable, with lots of lightly layered looks combining unexpected colors, volumes and textures in a way that somehow always works.

WWW.TOGA.JP

XANADU
This Harajuku select shop features up-and-coming Japanese designers, including red-hot lines DRESSEDUNDRESSED, Nyte and ROGGYKEI, plus fashioned-themed exhibitions.

WWW.XANADUTOKYO.COM

LIFT
16-5 Daikanyama-cho
Shibuya-ku, Tokyo
+81 (0) 3 3780 0163

MILK
6-29-3 Jingumae
Shibuya-ku, Tokyo
+81 (0) 3 5467 6555

MISTER HOLLYWOOD
4-13-16 Jingumae
Shibuya-ku, Tokyo
+81 (0) 3 5414 5071

PHENOMENON
CURRENT
Omotesando
4-26-21 Jingumae
Second Floor
Shibuya-ku, Tokyo
+81 (0) 3 5414 1634

SISTER
2F FAKE 18-4
Udagawa-cho
Shinjuku-ku, Tokyo
+81 (0) 3 5456 9892

SWAGGER
CURRENT
Omotesando
4-26-21 Jingumae
Shibuya-ku, Tokyo
+81 (0) 3 5414 1591

TOGA
Toga Harajuku
6-31-10 Jingumae
Shibuya-ku, Tokyo
+81 (0) 3 6419 8136

XANADU
4F Plaza F4 3-34-
7 Jingumae
Shibuya-ku Tokyo
+81 (0) 3 6459 2826

SWAGGER

NYTE

PHENOMENON

STOCKHOLM

1902 Luxury department store Nordiska Kompaniet opens in Stockholm

1947 Fast-fashion pioneer H&M opens its first store

1979 Swedish Fashion Council forms to promote local design

1996 Creative collective Acne forms

2000s "Det svenska modeundret" (the Swedish Fashion Wonder)
brings Stockholm style to the international stage

2002 Weekday opens weekend-only secondhand store outside of Stockholm

2005 Fashion Week by Berns inaugurated to showcase Swedish fashion

STOCKHOLM:
SCANDANAVIA'S COOL CAPITAL

BY ANDY CARLSON

Sweden can seem like an Astrid Lindgren fairytale, but the city of Stockholm throws the book at you. You don't have to look past the tarmac at the airport to find fantastical six-foot-tall men and women with chiseled features and inherent style. The Stockholm city center isn't much different. If you pop into a McDonalds, the girl asking if you would like ketchup with your fries is only moments away from being signed to a global modeling agency. The next time you see her will be in a magazine. Yet she's not just good looking. She tucks her uniform pants into fluorescent argyle socks, and flaunts a pair of one-of-a-kind studded Converse in her personal take on corporate America.

Even Stockholm's older generation looks like they jumped out of a Ralph Lauren ad. These thoroughbreds just got off their sailboat in fitted jeans and deck shoes after

navigating the Stockholm archipelago to find the perfect cove for
an afternoon swim (at least in summertime when the waters reach 70
degrees). When the younger generation isn't jumping off rocks into the
Baltic Sea, they stick to their specific
island neighborhoods, their own
creative sanctuaries. Stockholm is an
archipelago—a group of more than
1,800 islands and the larger islands
around the city center each contain
a specific culture, style and feeling.
There is no better way to observe the
local styles than through a tour of the
island neighborhoods of Stockholm.

Generally, Swedish culture seems
locked in by stereotypes such as social democracy, free healthcare and
IKEA. With those in place, freeing

up the population's time and money,
Stockholm becomes a machine for
creativity and design. This longtime
epicenter of Scandinavian design
has its 20th-century roots in afford-
able, functioning architecture and
interior design based on access
to inexpensive raw materials. This
access has made Sweden a world
outlet for minimalism. An obvious
example would the global expansion of IKEA and department store
H&M, which simply stands for
Hers and His, Hennes & Mauritz.

As for the other countries in the
Scandinavian design network—
Denmark, Norway and sometimes
Finland—only Sweden has found
a true global audience, and the
world keeps begging for more.

One consistent side effect of Swedish heritage is a fashion sense that maintains an allegiance to minimalism, and today's Swedish youth happily play with that tradition. Designers here preserve an air of modesty. As a result, a delightful sense of uniquely Scandinavian humor was born. A Swedish fashion designer will borrow functionality, deconstruct it, reinvent it, and deconstruct it again. For instance, the Italian designers at Diesel may take a vintage leather jacket and reconstruct it with an arbitrary screen print, several useless straps and call it "fashion." On the other hand, Fifth Avenue Shoe Repair, a frontrunner of Swedish design, will play with the onslaught of excess by attaching similar bells and whistles—a strap here, a faux collar there—and then they will remove the features, bringing the piece back down to its simplest form—a minimal look that echoes their various trials and experiments.

Unfortunately for the Swedes, they did not design Stockholm's archipelago, but of course they utilize the function of the separate islands. Each larger island within the metropolitan area has a corresponding neighborhood with a specific style. It's as if the Swedes decided in 1250 A.D.: Let's put the Vikings on one island, seamstresses here, the castle there, and the bathhouse over there. In the 21st century it's not much different: still divided, functional, creative, still awesome.

In the island of Södermalm, the hip, younger generation can watch their popular local musicians in high-end vintage fashion pieces, while by day

^ BACKSTAGE AT FILIPPA K

they produce their own boutique designs. By way of Östermalm, the Stockholm Brats (a laughable Swedish term for the aristocratic) can eat brunch in tailored shirts and fitted denim, while their wives, flaunting flowery summer dresses, cart around newborns and rap about their recent trip to IKEA. In Gamla Stan, the tourists can visit 800-year-old architecture and purchase postcards and Swedish novelties. If the fashion players stumble upon this centric isle they can visit the atelier castle of the iconic local label Acne.

At the center of these islands sits Stockholm's nucleus, its Times Square—Stureplan. Whether you're gallivanting in the dark with a bunch of rowdy artists looking for a secret DJ set by The Knife or finding your way back to your hotel carting bags from Weekday and Fifth Avenue Shoe Repair, you'll wind up passing through Stureplan.

Södermalm is the local hipster mecca; it's the Brooklyn of New York, the Silver Lake of L.A., the East End of London. Everything edgy is filtered through Södermalm's shores. You'll mostly find vintage here:

H&M

Established in 1947 as a low-priced clothier, Hennes & Mauritz has become Sweden's preeminent fast-fashion line. Known for their runway-reminiscent separates and trendy silhouettes for men, women and children, H&M defines their mission as, "fashion and quality at the best price." In addition to their clothing lines, the company also sells accessories, cosmetics, lingerie and home furnishings.

Already ubiquitous in America and Europe— their largest market is Germany—H&M recently opened up retail outlets in Japan, South Korea and the Middle East. With 2000 stores in 36 countries, and South American expansion in the works, this decade has seen H&M become a top global player of the most colorful kind.

In 2004, H&M's popularity was brought to a boil with their designer collection by Karl Lagerfeld, which sold out within the hour in many markets. Dedicated diffusion lines for H&M by Stella McCartney, Viktor & Rolf, Madonna, Roberto Cavalli, Comme des Garçons, Matthew Williamson, Jimmy Choo and Sonia Rykiel soon followed inspiring a new blend of discount-designer clothing soon copied by other brands.

These in-demand collaborations with high fashion designers helped H&M gain cache among fashionistas of a certain ilk, and increased revenues dramatically. Now, the influential business model of this Swedish megabrand is firmly on the rise, and fast-fashion fans could not be more thrilled.

For more information, or to find a store near you, visit **WWW.HM.COM**

boutiques with sarcastic names like Nitty Gritty and Beyond Retro, which offer classic designs from Chanel and Lanvin. Even the record store/nightclub called Pet Sounds (another stab at the Swede's awareness of Americana) serves up vintage vinyl and puts out hometown favorites. Södermalm revels in kitsch. Designers here idolize foreign styles, even as they play with them. The Södermalmers are not entirely against minimalism, but they don't make it their primary force. They'd rather sample sensational styles from around the world and reinterpret them for counterculture Swedish tastes.

Here you'll find Old Touch, an emporium of vintage Victorian-era lingerie for her and underwear for him. "Raggare" also comes to mind, the local community of Swedish greasers. Raggare is not Söderlmalm's only subculture, but it's the handiest example of how locals embrace and refine various foreign styles. It's like they hopped out of a time machine that left the United States in the 1950s and picked up some Hell's Angels along the way. The look requires a partial sleeve of tattoos, a quaffed haircut, an American muscle car blasting Hank Williams, and a leather jacket stating what crew or Swedish town you're from. There's no in-between with this niche culture. As with so much in Södermalm, you're either in or you're out.

Södermalm is vintage, but it is also inevitably Swedish. No matter how "punk" their fashion styles may appear, Swedes never give up their inherent allegiance to good design. Here you'll find Mississippi Inn, a

NK

Nordiska Kompaniet has been Stockholm's most luxurious fashion destination since it opened its doors in 1902. A traditional galleria spread over six floors, NK is Sweden's most elegant department store. It features the cream of the crop in fashion, accessories and home goods, and has been a favorite of Stockholm's most stylish residents—including the royal family—for generations.

NK is home to a mix of upper-crust luxury and cutting-edge design. The ground floor features a selection of traditional Swedish crystal, while the NK Nordiska Designers collection offers the likes of Whyred, Acne, Tiger and Back by Ann-Sofie Back. While the local looks are impressive, true fashion followers will want to check out the international collection as well, filled with luxurious garments from top international designers such as Prada, Vivienne Westwood and Givenchy.

All this shopping got you thirsty? Hit up NK's signature Champagne Bar to toast a day—and a few couple paychecks—well spent.

Hamngatan 18-20
Stockholm
+46 (0) 8 762 80 00
WWW.NK.SE

restaurant offering a Swedish take on Southern comfort food. It has all the trappings of a Tennessee steakhouse, however there's nothing Southern or dated about it. These Swedish chefs spend time designing detail when deconstructing famous foreign dinner plates. This goes for music as well. The neighborhood's sole venue, Debaser, houses acts such as the electronic phenomenon The Knife; the dance-y, full-suited new-school rockers The Hives, or mounds of global talent such as Lykke Li and Jose Gonzales. Here, you can watch Peter, Bjorn and John perform a personalized version of "Young Folks" in the evening, and then rub elbows with them at an apartment party thrown by the Shout Out Louds shortly after. If you get kicked out of the party for being too rowdy you can always set up shop in Benny Andersson's (of ABBA) Hotel Rival. Each room is dressed up by a local designer.

If for some odd reason you can't find a sailboat, hop on the subway. Only four stories below ground, it easily traverses the city islands with minimalist design and minimal noise. Feel free to use your cell phone or the Wi-Fi on your short trip; it's entirely included. And if you don't have cash, just don't pay. As long as you're young the Stockholm transportation authority will look the other way. They want you to be able to get where you're

going without punishment—a fruit of fully functioning social democracy.

It's a short subway ride over to Östermalm, the Beverly Hills of Stockholm, where the elite, the ad agencies, the digital design houses, the production companies, and the families reside. The cliché is good food, beautiful living space, and happy people. There really isn't anything too edgy about this neighborhood, just beautiful people modestly reveling in their success. If you look out the window on a sunny day, pretty much every female has a newborn baby. Groups of stroller-pushing moms move across the many tree-lined parks. The Södermalmers scoff at them, and vice versa. In Östermalm, the middle-aged

flaunt simple elegance. The styles you'll find here are more linear and consistent than the smörgåsbord of Södermalm. The Östermalmers stick to the labels, and casually wear new designs by Filippa K, J. Lindeberg, and Acne. Collared shirts, fitted jeans and long blond hair (guys and girls) are the standard. The Swedes have a term for these good-looking Östermalmers: Stockholm Brats. This culture might read as complacent when compared to the Södermalmers, but the trick here is when these Östermalmers go to work, they're bringing forward-leaning design to the rest of the world. They might keep the years of their youth packed away on a shelf holding their favorite punk vinyl, but it's likely they have had a part in designing that

specific shelf for brands like IKEA and Stockholm Design House. That same record shelf will show up in apartments around the world. With that solace Östermalmers rest easy, and bask, modestly of course.

If these Östermalmers are not at work or in the park, they're navigating through tourists on the picturesque island of Gamla Stan. This quaint island houses Old Town Stockholm, where you can find 800-year-old buildings including the king's castle. If you're looking to buy high-end design in this neighborhood, forget it. All you'll find are postcards of blonde women riding moose through forests and other Swedish tourist regalia. Gamla Stan is mostly known for indulging in Swedish novelty, but

the younger generation isn't going to let a prized panorama of their city be overrun by a tourist economy. Stockholm's hippest nightspot, Le Rouge, is located here, and houses the even more exclusive nightclub, Le Bar. Wear something weird, and tell them where you're from. They'll let you in. They love foreigners.

The design headquarters for Acne, Sweden's most successful fashion house, is located on Gamla Stan in a beautiful castle-like building that highlights their proud position as a global fashion line. Acne is extremely unique because it still falls under the Parisian guidelines of an atelier, such as the fashion houses that still operate out of Paris, names like Christian Dior and Chanel. Acne, however, is still young. Founded in 1996 by four friends, their fresh outlook allows Acne to avoid being labeled as only a clothing brand. Acne carries on their Swedish design lineage by developing a hyper-eclectic design house: a successful advertising agency, branding agency, film-production company as well as the magazine *Acne Paper* which biannually showcases coverage on international up-and-coming art and artists. Acne alone warrants a trip to Gamla Stan, but you're looking to taste a piece of each island you can stay within a four-block radius: Stureplan.

Stureplan is the nucleus of it all. This is the heart of Stockholm, the center of the baby-carting moms, the raw hipsters, the fumbling tourists and Swedish style. Stureplan is flanked not only by famous nightlife spots, but by famous design shops, one-of-a-kind hotels and globally distributed high-end fashion lines in the form of 100-square-foot boutiques. It is the city's fashion center.

Here, Acne Jeans has several boutiques that flank mall-sized H&M stores. Filippa K and J. Lindeberg—two staples of Swedish fashion—also have flagship stores along these cobbled streets. Weekday is a concept store where you can give your Östermalm suit from Filippa K a Södermalm twist. Every hot new line is filtered through Weekday, including Cheap Monday, the in-house denim line with roots in punk rock.

INDUSTRIAL DESIGN

If the Swedes had it their way, all humans would be born ready to construct an end table. Simplicity, function and affordability—these are the three tenets of Swedish industrial design. Innovation is also held in high regard, as long as it doesn't get in the way of practicality or sustainability, and stays user-friendly. Far from the trendy designs that fall out of fashion and need to be replaced, Sweden's well-conceived, purpose-driven creations are designed to last, and remain useful, for years to come.

The devotion to functionalism goes way back: *Modern Swedish Design*, an influential book published in 1899, is still in print, and the design association Svensk Form, formed in 1845 and the oldest organization of its kind in the world, also holds the distinction of being the first-ever publishers of a design magazine, *Form*, which arrived in 1905.

Now, the torch is being carried by Stockholm-based industrial designers like Björn Dahlström, Pia Wallén and Jonas Bohlin, as well as the popular IKEA chain, which cemented Sweden as the fifth largest European producer of ready-to-assemble furniture.

REQUIRED READING

RODEO Inspirational web magazine *Rodeo* is chock-full of colorful photographs, shopping suggestions, and hosts several excellent blogs. **WWW.RODEO.NET**

VICE SCANDINAVIA For quirky investigative articles and the best and worst of street style, head to *Vice Scandinavia*, which is conveniently in English.
WWW.VICELAND.COM/SE

BON *Bon* magazine is home to a coterie of roving style bloggers, who write, shoot high-quality fashion show videos and snap party pictures.
WWW.BONMAGAZINE.COM

VESTOJ The print journal of sartorial matters, *Vestoj*, contains academic writing about fashion and art, in the Queen's English. **WWW.VESTOJ.COM**

ELLE The most popular fashion glossy in Sweden, *ELLE* is required page flipping for those in search of the latest trends. The website is home to Filippa Berg's popular blog, Cinnamon Girl. **WWW.ELLE.SE**

ACNE PAPER The magazine from the creative collective behind Acne Jeans combines in-depth essays and provocative interviews with beautiful photography and cutting-edge fashion. **WWW.ACNEPAPER.COM**

Stureplan is also home to Fifth Avenue Shoe Repair, the fastest-rising fashion line from the Swedes. If any Swedish fashion line rivals Acne, this would be it. Fifth Avenue Shoe Repair carries two lines, ready-to-wear and the couture-inspired By the No.

All Sweden's functionality, social democracy and general happiness has an intense side effect: At night the city catches fire. There's no better place for partying than Stureplan. Most "cool" Stockholmers won't call Stureplan their first choice for nightlife but it is the default mecca, the Stockholm that doesn't sleep.

At the southern end of Stureplan is Berns, a highly ornate hotel located in a park.

∧ STUREPAN

Only the flashy stay here, but you'll find yourself easily admitted to their nightly parties. If for some reason you don't meet any friends, you can also play blackjack inside the club. A few blocks up is Café Opera, another bourgie nightclub that also houses the Nobel Prize Awards after-party.

When you arrive at the center of Stureplan, you'll know. It's a huge square that's home to hotels such as Scandic Anglais, Story Hotel and nightclubs and restaurants Sturecompagniet, Sturehof, Riche and the infamous Spy Bar—all across the street from each other within a triangle. You will be let in to all of them, but, in something

of a Swedish rite of passage, you'll probably be thrown out of Spy Bar.

Notoriously housed in a mansion of sorts, Spy Bar is a maze of rooms, caverns and playhouses. There may be a goth show in one room, and the The Hives spinning in another.

The moment you're having too much fun, you will be asked to leave Spy Bar on the grounds of reckless behavior. They do this in order to keep filtering in more paying customers.

Don't fret, you'll be immortalized on the MySpace page in broken English: Spy Bar Throwed Me Out.

NEIGHBORHOODS

SÖDERMALM
The island of Södermalm is where the creative and fashionable go to dine, imbibe and purchase vintage garb. Fittingly, this former working class neighborhood was the birthplace of Greta Garbo, and has some of the prettiest buildings in the capital.

GAMLA STAN
Historic Gamla Stan, or Old Town, is made up of gorgeous cobblestoned streets, landmark buildings, quaint shops and, inevitably, loads of tourists and Viking souvenirs. Moose handicrafts aside, Gamla Stan is a lovely place for a beer or a stroll.

ÖSTERMALM
Östermalm's Stureplan is the place where socialites and hipsters play together nicely. This public square connects three major thoroughfares and boasts trendy bars and designer shops, as well as fancy hotels and exclusive restaurants.

NORRMALM
There is a wealth of pedestrian shopping streets in Norrmalm, the commercial hub around Central Station. Here is where the famous King's Garden lies.

SKEPPSHOLMEN
Many museums are located on small and scenic Skeppsholmen Island, such as the Modern Museum, the Museum of Architecture and the Museum of Far Eastern Antiquities. The National Museum is located near the bridge leading to the island.

< GAMLA STAN

HOTSPOTS

LE ROUGE
The decadently decorated Gamla
Stan restaurant Le Rouge—and
the neighboring watering hole
Le Bar—are crowded homes
to Stockholm's hipsters.

Brunnsgränd 2
Stockholm
+46 (0) 8 505 244 30
WWW.LEROUGE.SE

THE SPY BAR
Upscale Östermalm club Spy
Bar has seen its share of
celebrities, musicians and raucous
behavior. The vibe is dress to
impress and be prepared to
spend some serious krona.

Birger Jarlsgatan 20
Stockholm
+46 (0) 8 5450 37 04
WWW.THESPYBAR.COM

STORY HOTEL
Stockholm's trendiest hotel features
a lively restaurant and laid-back
bar, as well as a selection of artfully
designed rooms and suites where
the jet set recharge amid a charming
selection of contemporary art.

Riddargatan 6
Stockholm
+46 (0) 8 545 039 40
WWW.STORYHOTELS.COM

< LE ROUGE

SWEDEN'S IT GIRL
FILIPPA BERG

Style icon and blogger Filippa Berg has received all sorts of accolades in her homeland, from "It" girl of the year in 2008 to best dressed of 2009 (both by ELLE magazine). Her signature look—at once girly and playful—has made her an international style icon, and muse for labels such as Los Angeles-based Wren, which featured her in their fall 2009 look book.

But the Stockholm native, who spent her formative years backpacking around Europe and North Africa with her parents, has a healthy and realistic view of the fashion aquarium in which she lives and works.

WHAT'S YOUR INVOLVEMENT IN STOCKHOLM'S FASHION SCENE?
I work as a freelance fashion stylist and writer. I do a very popular fashion blog for Swedish *ELLE*, called Cinnamon Girl. I have been in the industry since my early teens when I began my somehow successful model career. I left modeling at 22 and started to assist one of Sweden's leading stylists, Karin Smeds.

WHAT MAKES SWEDISH STYLE SO APPEALING?
It's wearable, practical, semi-edgy and full of clean cuts.

EVERYONE IN STOCKHOLM LOOKS GREAT, BUT MANY ARE DRESSED SIMILARLY. WHY DO YOU THINK THAT IS?
Because people here are anxious about fashion. Fashion is as big in Stockholm

as MTV was in the '90s. Everybody wants or thinks that they have to be part of it, but many don't really know just how to do it. That's why they buy the uniform. To feel fashionably safe. I say, if you are not interested, why bother? There are so many other great things in the world apart from fashion!

WHAT IS YOUR PERSONAL STYLE? HOW HAS IT EVOLVED THROUGH-OUT THE YEARS?
My style is a mixture of me and a Californian exchange student in Paris 1969. I started to dress in only vintage when I was 14 and since then I have found a lot of great stuff. That, together with experience, has made my style more and more refined every year. But all together, the concept remains the same.

THERE IS A HUGE FOCUS ON TREND CONSCIOUS WEARABILITY IN SWEDEN. HOW DID THAT COME ABOUT?
I think it's because of the weather here and the practical Swedish soul. People want to look like they are smart and aware of what's happening, but at the same time they don't want to stand out from the crowd. It all has to do with the Swedish expression *lagom*, which means, "just in the middle". It's very important to be *lagom* … but I don't give a damn about that of course.

For more style tips from Stockholm's It-girl visit Filippa's blog at
WWW.ELLE.SE/BLOGGAR/ FILIPPA-BERGS-BLOGG.ASPX

FILIPPA'S PICKS

It has a stupid name, but the SoFo area in Södermalm is where you'll find Acne, the great art book store Konst-ig, and second-hand shop Stadsmissionen. It's also home to Lisa Larsson—the best vintage store in town—Tjallamalla, a boutique filled with young Swedish designers and Pet Sounds, the best record store in town.

Another great area is Krukmakargatan in Södermalm, where you'll find Nitty Gritty and Papercut, the best place for fashion magazines.

Acne
WWW.ACNE.SE

Konst-ig
WWW.KONSTIG.SE

Stadsmissionen
WWW.STADSMISSIONEN.SE

Lisa Larsson
LISALARSSONSECONDHAND.COM

Tjallamalla
WWW.TJALLAMALLA.COM

Pet Sounds
WWW.PETSOUNDS.SE

Nitty Gritty
WWW.NITTYGRITTY.SE

Papercut
WWW.PAPERCUTSHOP.SE

COPENHAGEN

The nations of Scandinavia share more than a chilly climate. Each is also known for a love of crisp and clean design that extends to fashion, furniture and even architecture. It's no wonder then that Stockholm's neighbor, Copenhagen, is itself emerging as a fashion capital. The Danish capital has hosted its own fashion week since 1964, when it was called the Scandinavian Fashion Fair. Five decades later, the city has developed its own signature style—a fashion-forward look steeped in the tradition of color and craft. What further sets the city apart is its focus on wearable, youthful clothing, which means the dress you see on the runway is all the more likely to show up on the street. While Copenhagen style scene is still overlooked compared to its more established neighbors, the city is gaining momentum. Cheap Monday chose Copenhagen over its native Stockholm as the location for its first store, and its sidewalks are a favorite of street style photographers. The city itself is also looking toward a fashionable future—its Fall 2010 shows were live streamed on giant screens at City Hall.

^ CHEAP MONDAY, COPENHAGEN

^ SCENES FROM COPENHAGEN FASHION WEEK

WOOD WOOD

STINE GOYA

HENRIK VIBSKOV

HENRIK VIBSKOV
Perhaps no designer personifies Copenhagen fashion more than Henrik Vibskov, a graduate of London's Central St. Martins whose fanciful garments come in bright colors and innovative shapes that lie somewhere between streetwear and the avant-garde.
Krystalgade 6
Copenhagen
+45 33 14 61 00
WWW.HENRIKVIBSKOV.COM

LOUISE AMSTRUP
Louise Amstrup's modern designs combine bold digital prints with solid pieces in black, white and gray for a look at that's equal parts sexy and powerful.
WWW.LOUISE-AMSTRUP.COM

STINE GOYA
Stine Goya makes sophisticated, feminine clothing with playful details in a rich palette of saturated colors.
WWW.STINEGOYA.COM

NOIR
While its luxurious aesthetic treads on fashion's darker edges, Noir mixes an erotic sensibility with a dedication to corporate social responsibility.
WWW.NOIR-ILLUMINATI2.COM

WOOD WOOD
Three-man fashion collective Wood Wood grew from a T-shit label into full-on streetwear brand, creating highly sought after limited-edition sneaker collaborations along the way.
Krystalgade 7
Copehagen
+45 3393 6264
WWW.WOODWOOD.DK

ACNE

Creative collective Acne extends far beyond fashion into advertising, film and the magazine *Acne Paper*. In addition to its premium denim, the label features refined, intelligent cuts. **WWW.ACNEJEANS.COM**

ANN-SOFIE BACK

After ten years of working in London, Ann-Sofie Back recently took the helm at Cheap Monday. Her solo label remains one of unexpected depth, imagination and glamour. **WWW.ANNSOFIEBACK.COM**

BURFITT

Illustrator Lovisa Burfitt combines art and fashion to create exciting clothes which run the gamut from theatrical to somber to romantic. **WWW.BURFITT.COM**

CARIN WESTER

Carin Wester's clothing for men and women combines sustainable materials with a minimalist color palate and seasonless shapes for looks that are cool, but never trendy. **WWW.CARINWESTER.COM**

CHEAP MONDAY

The low-cost label that launched the skinny Swedish jeans craze recently enlisted the dark sensibilities of Ann-Sofie Back for its expanded range of wallet-friendly duds. **WWW.CHEAPMONDAY.COM**

DAVID & MARTIN

Karl Lagerfeld collaborators David & Martin create some of Stockholm's most in-demand jewelry in shapes such as chicken feet, bones and numbers. **WWW.DAVIDANDMARTIN.COM**

FILIPPA K

One would be hard-pressed to find anything disagreeable at Filippa K, a label featuring stylish, practical and form-fitting staples, designed for sophisticated professionals. **WWW.FILIPPA-K.COM**

HOPE

Ann Ringstrand and Stefan Söderberg find inspiration in vintage menswear and uniforms for looks that are consistently clean and timeless. **HOPE-STHLM.COM**

ACNE

ANN-SOFIE BACK

CARIN WESTER

HOUSE OF DAGMAR

Started by three sisters who named the label after their grandmother, the unabashedly girly House of Dagmar favors tight-fitting dresses, suits and jackets, provocative lingerie elements and flirty floral dresses.

WWW.HOUSEOFDAGMAR.SE

IDA SJÖSTEDT

Elegant kitsch is the order of the day at Ida Sjöstedt, where frills, lace and transparent gauze rule in spring and colorful, texturized garments reign in fall.

WWW.IDASJOSTEDT.COM

J. LINDEBERG

Sportswear meets masculine glamour at J. Lindeberg, one of Sweden's most famous labels. In the brand's stores, tuxedos, tailored suiting and golf gear all hang side by side.

WWW.JLINDEBERG.COM

MARTIN BERGSTRÖM

The striking creations of textile artist Martin Bergström, are highly prized among fashionistas. He describes his intricate designs as "organic futurism," often made using French Revolution-era construction techniques.

MARTINBERGSTROM.COM

SANDRA BACKLUND

Based in tradition, but also cutting-edge, Sandra Backlund's intricate, handcrafted knitwear explores the limits of fabric, texture and the more sculptural side of fashion.

SANDRABACKLUND.COM

STORES

ACNE
Norrmalmstorg 2
Stockholm
+46 (0) 8 611 64 11

CARIN WESTER
Rörstrandsgatan 24
Stockholm
+46 (0) 8 30 54 15

DAVID & MARTIN
Hökensgata 5
Stockholm
+46 (0) 8 650 32 65

FILIPPA K
Grev Turegatan 18
Stockholm
+46 (0) 8 678 65 00

HOPE
Norrlandsgatan 12
Stockholm
+46 (0) 8 678 11 30

J. LINDEBERG
Biblioteksgatan 6
Stockholm
+46 (0) 8 4005 00 41

CHEAP MONDAY

FILIPPA K

HOPE

SYDNEY

SYDNEY STYLE

BY PAUL BUI

On the opposite hemisphere to the fashion capitals of the world, Sydney appears an unlikely player in the fashion game. But like the diversity of its multicultural people, this melting-pot city offers a wide diversity of aesthetics, and has, over its short history, created a distinct style of its own. While some may suggest that Australia tends to borrow too much from European trends, there are a few local labels and designers that have placed their own stamp on Sydney style. And of course there's

∧ (LEFT) MC GAFF E AT KSUBI'S BIG IN JAPAN PARTY; (TOP) THE TOY TOY PARTY AT LADY LUX;
  (BOTTOM) BACKSTAGE AT KIRRILY JOHNSTON RAFW
< (PREVIOUS SPREAD) SYDNEY HARBOUR BRIDGE

the lifestyle; it's hard to imagine what Sydney fashion would look like if it weren't for the prevailing beach culture and scantily dressed women.

Claimed by Great Britain as a penal colony in 1770, Australia didn't have such a steeped and illustrious relationship with high fashion as its European or even American counterparts. For decades, Australian fashion did not really have a distinct identity. This changed with the work of Sydneysiders Jenny Kee and Linda Jackson. Unlike their predecessors, who often replicated European trends and designs, Kee and Jackson embraced Australiana with colorful gusto. While their designs may be considered kitsch now, during the mid 1970s Kee and Jacksons' knits depicting Australian emblems, such as koalas and gumnuts, proved to be roaring success

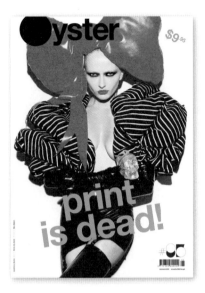

scoring editorial spreads in revered publications around the globe.

Nowadays, designers such as buzzed-about Romance Was Born, a line designed by Luke Sales and Anna Plunkett, take cues from Kee and Jackson, showcasing collections that reference the Australian environment, through prints based on Australian art and maps. Other labels such as Ksubi and Lover started off in beachside Bondi, inspired by their surroundings, only to become major success stories.

Bondi is without a doubt Sydney's most well known suburb. Its world-famous beach, shops, bars and res-

taurants attract thousands of tourists a year. While some may argue that the inner-city surburbs of Paddington and Surry Hills are much more fashion-forward, Sydney's beaches still impact the city's style, playing muse to many designers as well as the masses on the sidewalk.

"Beach culture is what makes Sydney clothing so scant, to show off beach-ready bodies and tans," observes Alyx Gorman, Associate Editor

^ *OYSTER* MAGAZINE; SYDNEY STREET SCENE

casual wear, work wear and even denim labels such as Ksubi, one of Australia's leading denim labels. The brand launched over ten years ago when two surfers from Bondi, Dan Single and George Gorrow, dragged their jeans behind a (delightfully retro) Kingswood car to get that "worn in" effect. The brand has since become a runaway success. A pair of Ksubi jeans was the must-have item for discerning fashion fans during the naughties. And it's no surprise that Sydney's beaches were a source of inspiration.

"Our designs are derived from our lifestyle, which includes elements of the Australian beach, sun and surf," Single says. "Just like the environment, we are constantly evolving." Since its 2000 launch, Ksubi has become one of Australia's most prominent cult fashion brands, whilst maintaining that elusive core of "cool." The brand is stocked all around the world and serves for many as an introduction to Australian fashion, a movement Single describes as: "forward-thinking, with a touch of irony, humor and color".

Lover is another label that started in Bondi only to become an overseas sensation. Known for their cute but adventurous designs, Lover

of Australia's oldest independent fashion publication, *Oyster* magazine. "The beach is ever-present, even in eveningwear. It's what decides our color palettes (intended to show off tans, and to reflect the brightness of the sun) and it's generally the surf-y labels that do really well, especially for mainstream and high-street consumers."

Beach culture doesn't just influence swimwear in Sydney. It influences

REQUIRED READING

Magazines

VOGUE AUSTRALIA
Australia's answer to *Vogue* features high-end fashion with a local twist. The magazine made news in June 2010 by putting Aboriginal model Samantha Harris on the cover.
WWW.VOGUE.COM.AU

OYSTER
Out-there styling and features on the next waves of music and fashion pioneers make *Oyster* one of Australia's most exciting magazines.
WWW.OYSTERMAG.COM

RUSSH
Bi-monthly fashion magazine *Russh* features cutting-edge fashion, music, art and film, with lush photography and inspirational styling for fashion-forward readers.
WWW.RUSSHMAGAZINE.COM

FRANKIE
A bimonthly magazine with a sweet take on art, fashion, crafts and culture.
WWW.FRANKIE.COM.AU

YEN MAGAZINE
Indie magazine *Yen* is young, fun and totally trendy, with articles that tackles social, political and cultural issues with a positive perspective and a little bit of attitude. **WWW.YENMAG.NET**

SHOP 'TIL YOU DROP
Shopping tips, runway-to-real-way fashion spreads and other inspiration for everyday style.
WWW.SHOPTILYOUDROP.COM.AU

started off at Bondi Markets in 2001 with partners Susien Chong and Nic Briand selling their wares to passersby. These days, the brand is championed by celebrities such as Kate Hudson and Kirsten Dunst and stocked in Europe, the United States and Asia.

"We started with a clear idea that we would be a boutique brand of international standard," Chong and Briand say. "Living in Australia was not going to be an excuse for poor quality and old ideas. We wanted to hang on the racks next to labels we admired, with a reference to where we came from. We are very proud of Australia's culture and have always woven that into our label. Whether it be film, art or music, it's all in there."

With a strong sense of pride in where they come from, Chong and Briand find inspiration from a uniquely local

point of view. "Your environment has to become an influence," they explain. "For example, our swimwear isn't just inspired by the beach; it's mainly inspired by teens jumping into creeks and sitting in suburban above-ground pools, killing time. It's not about the bronzed 'Aussie'—but we have always maintained that that isn't the only kind of 'Aussie'."

With original designers such as Lover and Ksubi, this modern Aussie style—and, more specifically, Sydney style—is forging a path of its very own, and becoming a clear concept along the way. Briand and Chong describe the local look as "a true re-flection of the city in itself—Sydney is a young, multicultural city, which comes across in attitudes, architec-ture and the people. Many will say

that the Sydney style is 'relaxed' due to the beach lifestyle, and that is partly true, but drive for 30 minutes away from the beach and you have run-down, inner-city warehouses and Chinese tea houses, which are the complete opposite of beach culture. And that is the beauty of the city."

Oyster magazine's Gorman has her own definition: "I think different parts of Sydney all have their own unique styles—but if you had to label the whole city, the look would, without question, be 'sexy.' As it is with most beachside, sunny cities, Sydney's style is very much about showing off flesh. One of the first things people comment on when they arrive is how scantily dressed Sydney women are—regardless of subculture—and one of the first things people notice

when they leave is how much more conservatively women in Europe dress. Sydney has tossed aside the 'show one part of your body' and instead favours body-con micro-minis with plunging necklines."

In every city, the fashion sub-set has their uniforms, though it changes with the tides of time, of course. So if kids in London's Shoreditch sport experimental get-ups with colorful trimmings and New York's Williamsburg set is still rocking the double denim, Sydney also has her fail-safe outfit that she'll often pull out of her wardrobe. "In Sydney you really cannot go past a little jersey dress," says Gorman. "They are comfortable, unwrinklable and can be dressed

up or down to suit season, trends and occasion. For day, it can work with sandals, ballet flats or brogues, and a bangle or long pendant, and then in the evening you can throw on some high heels and earrings, and you're aces." For the boys, says Single, the go-to is "jeans, an old T-shirt and leather jacket (if it's cold). It's a perfect day and night outfit."

Likewise, every city will have designers that help shape its identity. In Sydney, these stalwarts range from aforementioned pioneers such as Jenny Kee and Linda Jackson to more recent innovators such as Ksubi and Lover. Other designers who have made a significant impact on Australian

^ ROMANCE WAS BORN DESIGNERS LUKE SALES AND ANNA PLUNKETT

fashion include Collette Dinnigan, Sass & Bide, Zimmermann, Willow, Josh Goot and Toni Maticevski. But with all the challenges young designers face these days, is it getting more difficult to make an impact beyond Australia? Perhaps, according to Lover designers Chong and Briand.

"Young Australian labels are far more sophisticated these days in terms of their presentation and confidence—even the business side has evolved. However, the biggest difficulty will always be cash for growth, and how rapidly it is needed. Australian fashion just doesn't have the backbone in manufacturing and financial support that European and American designers have. When

^ (TOP) MODEL RACHEL RUTT OUTSIDE ROMANCE WAS BORN RAFW '10; MODEL LARA BINGLE FRONT ROW AT KSUBI RAFW '10

REQUIRED READING
Blogs

FROCKWRITER
Veteran fashion writer Patty Huntington reports from fashion's front lines.
WWW.FROCKWRITER.BLOGSPOT.COM

STYLELINES
Melbourne-based journalist Kat George is one of the web's most popular independent fashion bloggers, with her keen sense of style, great writing and strong opinions.
WWW.STYLELINES.BLOGSPOT.COM

IMELDA: THE DESPOTIC QUEEN OF SHOES
Named for the First Lady with a footwear fetish, Imelda covers Aussie fashion from the ground up.
WWW.IMELDA.COM.AU

SASSYBELLA
Since 2002, Helen Lee's blog has covered the best in fashion news and gossip. **WWW.SASSYBELLA.COM**

PEDESTRIAN
Fashion and pop culture news with a hip Australian angle.
WWW.PEDESTRIAN.TV

TWOTHOUSAND
A weekly webguide to the best of Sydney.
WWW.TWOTHOUSAND.COM.AU

GIRL WITH A SATCHEL
Erica Bartle offers a girly take on style, featuring interviews and magazine reviews.
WWW.GIRLWITHASATCHEL.BLOGSPOT.COM

those designers transmit their ideas, it is on a world stage. When young Australian designers do it, it can feel like they are at the bottom of the hill, and the climb will be a long one." In addition to these challenges, there is also the fact that Australia is still a very young country and its weather and seasons are opposite to those in the Northern Hemisphere. Logistically, this causes many problems for local designers selling overseas and causes insinuations that Aussie designers tend to copy from the overseas collections of prior seasons. But designers here dismiss such claims.

"I believe Australian fashion holds its own," Single says. "We tend to operate on our own schedule. We don't follow the seasonal rules and end up with collections that are irreverent and honest."

"It's true that we do have a lot stacked against us; the odds don't look so good," Chong and Briand admit. "But we have learnt that people will always recognize intelligent design no matter where it comes from. And when you want to compete on an international stage, you have to bring something different to the mix that is partly about where you are from. People know what they want from a designer in Belgium—and the same goes for Australia."

^ THERESE RAWSTHORNE BACKSTAGE AT RAFW '09

In the end, it is that desire for a distinctly Australian voice that drives our design talent and makes Australian fashion and Sydney style so appealing. It's true that our warm climate and beach culture are contributing factors, but it is through our talented designers and stylish citizens that a true identity—however young and however eclectic—is formed.

"The best thing about Sydney fashion is the sense of fun and playfulness," *Oyster* magazine's Gorman says. "It's great to live in a city where people will wear things sometimes because they are aware it looks silly, and really enjoy it for that. Sydney fashion is also very casual, which actually forces you to consider what you are wearing more than somewhere where black-tie events are com-

mon. Anyone can throw on a suit or a cocktail frock, but it takes deep deliberation to come up with an excellent casual-dressy ensemble."

As more and more Australian designers find international success, the momentum only grows, both here and abroad. "Someone like Collette Dinnigan did a show in Paris, and it blew all our minds that someone from Australia could do that," say Chong and Briand. "Zimmermann sold their swimwear to Victoria's Secret and proved that we could mix it with overseas labels. Then labels like Lover and Ksubi went over to New York and mingled with press and downtown kids and we realized we had a unique point of view. People want to know about that."

NEIGHBORHOODS

CIRCULAR QUAY
Circular Quay is the center of Sydney Harbour, home to the world-famous Opera House and many of the city's tourist attractions.

KING'S CROSS
Sydney's famous red-light district, King's Cross is a downtown neighborhood that's still a little gritty but with a growing number of trendy cafes, boutiques and record shops.

DARLINGTON
Upscale and home to the Oxford Street stretch of nightlife, Darlington is also home to Sydney's LGBT community.

PADDINGTON
The ritzy boutiques lining Oxford Street, the cafes of Five Ways and the offbeat offerings of Paddington Markets make this eastern suburb a shopper's dream.

BONDI
Perhaps Sydney's most famous spot, Bondi is one of the world's most beautiful beaches, and home to a laidback surfer vibe.

SURRY HILLS
Once a tough neighborhood, this Inner East suburb is one of Sydney's most fashionable neighborhoods, with an eclectic mix of cafés, restaurants and shops, plus a diverse population and thriving arts scene.

WATERLOO
Like neighboring Surry Hills, Waterloo has experienced a massive transformation, trading industrial warehouses for chic restaurants, and the 2 Danks Street gallery complex.

NEWTOWN
Punky and grungy, this Inner West suburb is quickly shedding its bad reputation, thanks in part to the students from nearby Sydney University who give the neighborhood an artsy vibe and edgy style.

< BELINDA BOUTIQUE, PADDINGTON

HOTSPOTS

NORTH BONDI ITALIAN FOOD
Italian cuisine is served in a cheerful yellow dining room on a sexy stretch of fashionable North Bondi beach.
120 Ramsgate Avenue
North Bondi, NSW
+61 (02) 9300 4400
WWW.IDRB.COM

THE CRICKETERS ARMS
The Crix, as it's called, is a laid-back pub that caters to the eclectic young crowd of Surry Hills. Grab a wintertime seat by the fire or head upstairs to escape the crowds and enjoy some tapas.
106 Fitzroy Street
Surry Hills, NSW
+61 (02) 9331 3301
WWW.MYSPACE.COM/
CRICKETERSARMSHOTEL

THE FLINDERS HOTEL
The historic hotel has reopened as a good ol' fashioned dive bar, a grungy—and crowded— hangout for Sydney hipsters.
63 Flinders Street
Darlinghurst, NSW
+61 (02) 9356 3622
WWW.THEFLINDERSHOTEL.COM.AU

PADDINGTON MARKETS
This outdoor market is where some of Sydney's biggest labels got their start, including Collette Dinnigan and Zimmermann. Every Saturday—rain or shine—it's where you can spot the next big thing.
395 Oxford Street
Paddington, NSW
+61 (02) 9331 2923
WWW.PADDINGTONMARKETS.COM.AU

< AN *OYSTER* MAGAZINE WAREHOUSE PARTY

STYLE EXPERT
KIT WILLOW

Kit Willow creates the type of clothing women want to wear—strong and structured, feminine, flattering and never boring. Though she has shown at both New York Fashion Week and Rosemount Australian Fashion Week, Australia is definitely home for this Melbourne native. In fact, the local environment can be seen directly in her designs—including a trip to the Great Barrier Reef that turned up on the runway in the form of relaxed tunics in deeps blue prints, nautilus shapes and sea-shell encrusted silhouettes.

^ DESIGNER KIT WILLOW AND LOOKS FROM HER AUTUMN/WINTER 2010/2011 ECLIPSE COLLECTION

HOW WOULD YOU DESCRIBE WILLOW?
Edgy femininity, architectural
psyche, technical style.

WHERE IS THE LABEL BASED?
Based in Sydney with three boutiques: one
in Paddington and two in Melbourne, one at
Melbourne's GPO and one in Hawksburn.

**YOUR CLOTHES ARE CONSISTENTLY FEMININE
AND FLATTERING; SOFT, BUT WITH AN EDGE.
WHAT TYPE OF WOMAN DO YOU HAVE
IN MIND WHEN YOU DESIGN?**
I believe in designing clothes for women
that want to be worn—to be inspired by
and just feel great wearing—day or night.

**YOUR WORK FREQUENTLY REFERENCES
NATURE—BIRDS, FLOWERS, WOOD AND
COLORS INSPIRED BY THE GREAT BARRIER
REEF. COULD YOU TELL ME A BIT ABOUT THAT?**
I think nature is the best creator in the
world; I am constantly fascinated and
inspired by the functionality, color and
form—everything nature has to offer.

WHERE DO YOU GO TO FIND INSPIRATION?
London. I love galleries, markets,
books, people and nature.

**OUR BOOK IS INTERESTED IN THE
WAYS PEOPLE EXPRESS THEMSELVES
THROUGH FASHION AROUND THE WORLD.
HOW WOULD YOU DESCRIBE SYDNEY
STYLE? IS THERE A "SYDNEY LOOK"?**
Quite "fashion" focused, a mix bag of
designer with sarong and thongs!

**YOU HAVE SHOPS IN BOTH SYDNEY
AND MELBOURNE. HOW DO THE TWO
CITIES COMPARE STYLE-WISE?**
I believe Melbourne has a lot more style,
but I am a Melbourne girl! Art and architecture define Melbourne style, while a
relaxed beach culture defines Sydney style.

For more on Willow visit
WWW.WILLOWLTD.COM

SOUTHERN STYLE
MELBOURNE

Sydney's southern neighbor, Melbourne, with its cooler climate, is home to a fashion scene with a darker sensibility than Sydney's beachy looks. It's also home to the prestigious Royal Melbourne Institute of Technology, which trains Australia's next generation of fashion designers. Nadia Napreychikov and Cami James, two recent RMIT grads, founders of the DI$COUNT label and its wildly popular blog, gave us the scoop the city's renegade style.

WHAT IS DI$COUNT ALL ABOUT AND WHAT IS YOUR MISSION?
DI$COUNT is the merging of our hearts and minds that allows us to articulate our passion for what we do and share it with anyone else who cares. To define it in business terms, DI$COUNT would be classified as a fashion label. We came up with DI$COUNT because we refused to change our ideals to fit into the current fashion system. DI$COUNT allows us freedom. We're designing our own place in the system and it's through the subversion of the fashion framework, that it was developed. The output is steeped in humor and irony, cliché and imitation. We are a luxury brand that doesn't only cater to the traditional luxury consumer.

HOW WOULD YOU DESCRIBE YOUR PERSONAL STYLES?
For us, the definition of "style" has little to do with clothing. Style is an intrinsic char-

^ A LOOK BY NADIA NAPREYCHIKOV

acteristic, it's the way you do something, it's your approach. Our personal approach to dressing doesn't really have anything to do with the clothes we wear or one particular item, it isn't something you can see, but rather something you can sense or feel. It is energy, and having a certain presence, and it's not something that can be bought. Style is a form of seduction, and you can seduce someone whilst wearing nothing at all!

HOW WOULD YOU DESCRIBE THE "MELBOURNE LOOK"?

If we are talking a specific Melbourne stereotype, then there is of course the black, asymmetrical, textured, layered, half-grunge, half-refined, "I'm a poet" look. Hopefully this one won't stick

around too long, because a lot of the time it comes with a shit attitude.

HOW DOES IT COMPARE WITH SYDNEY?

The majority of Australia's creative industry and the businesses that support this industry are based in Sydney. This leaves Melbourne with a bit of a void that has been filled with an unbridled creativity and a heap of passionate kids. People here aren't that interested in labels; it's more about the attitude and conviction. People are a lot more open here to experimentation, customization and creating something from nothing. Melbourne is like the dirty little brother with a smirk and sticky hands. Sydney is the polished older brother, with business cards, a white smile and a suit.

MORE AND MORE FASHION IS WINDING UP ON THE WEB. DO YOU THINK THIS DIGITAL COMMUNITY IS AFFECTING FASHION? HOW SO?
Through use of the internet, we gain access to rest of the world instantly; it closes the gap between trends in what are considered the "fashion meccas" of the world and our own local trends. We're increasingly moving towards larger-scale global trends because information is so instantly passed through channels around the world. Through online retail, and the ability to buy from anywhere in the world, we're now able to choose season/trend/culture/style—regardless of location. The fashion market has been cut up the guts, and the playing field is much vaster and more diverse than ever before, though simultaneously, it has created even ground. Money is not nearly as huge of an advantage where it used to be. To start up a conventional label you need capital (for maintaining retail space, stock, etc.); by using the net, anyone can enter the market and gain interest and momentum through the use of various online communication systems. There are, of course, many well known celebrities, blogs and labels that have succeeded from cash and access not talent...it just gives a better voice and platform to the little guy.

The evolution of the online consumer has superseded the industry's pace. In essence, we recognize that the traditional fashion system lags even in comparison to the counterfeit one. If you acknowl-

^ A LOOK BY CAMI JAMES

edge that collections are designed (give or take) six months before the images of them are released and then available for purchase a further six months later, it becomes transparent that with the evolution of the web and democratization of citizen journalism in the form of the blog, that this system is outdated.

If you compare this to how these images were originally distributed in the form of magazines and certain authoritative websites, it is important to acknowledge that the amount of outlets that have now become available for this dissemination has multiplied beyond belief, resulting in infinite saturation of the trend. It is not uncommon that imitation products are released even before the initial design. We all know what happened to the infamous Balmain jacket, the images were released months before the physical jacket was available, and then Zara and Topshop copies were retailed even before the original. The internet is propelling the organic, traditional flow of fashion, and it's eclipsing the system it exists in.

LET'S TALK INFLUENCES...ROCK 'N' ROLL IS OBVIOUSLY A BIG ONE. WHAT ARE YOU INTO RIGHT NOW?

Rock 'n' roll is definitely an influence, but not in terms of a music genre, or even the aesthetic of rock 'n' roll... it has everything to do with the attitude of it. Aesthetics fade and change, they are constantly evolving,

^ (CENTER AND ABOVE) STYLED BY DI$COUNT

but there is nothing more influential than watching someone with a genuine fire for what they believe in. If they can get a hold of your psyche, then it's completely captivating. Whether it be a musician, artist, designer or whoever, if they are utterly involved and have that frenzy, love, craziness for what they do, then it's electrifying to watch. It makes you feel you can do it too, seeing that fire in them.

^ A LOOK BY NADIA NAPREYCHIKOV

IS IT A GOOD TIME TO BE YOUNG AND CREATIVE IN MELBOURNE?

Absolutely. Melbourne is traditionally the cultural and creative capital of Australia. There are endless amounts of people willing to support creative talent and in turn this makes for the perfect place to start. It's a really nurturing atmosphere because people have a genuine interest in the creative arts; if you are willing to talk, they will listen. You can't be creative in a vacuum, for your work to be valid it needs to have a context and a small place like Melbourne is a great place to learn to exercise your voice.

ARE THERE ANY LOCAL DESIGNERS YOU WISH GOT MORE INTERNATIONAL ATTENTION?

Yeah, DI$COUNT! It is easy right now to get international attention if you really want it. If designers today choose to ignore this fantastic new avenue that we have to international recognition—the World Wide Web—then it's easy enough to say that they are quite content with simply continuing in the local market. It's all there for the taking, and if designers aren't willing to use it, then they probably don't necessarily deserve it. It's not a secluded world...we as Australian designers don't have the excuse of being too far away geographically anymore. It's all about wanting something and then going out and getting it. These days you can't wait for someone else to talk about you, you have to start the conversation. No excuses.

ANY TIPS FOR STYLE SAVVY PEOPLE VISITING MELBOURNE?

Melbourne is the kind of city you need to explore on foot and tram, all the best shops, bars and cafes are, as the reputation goes, hidden down lane ways. Get lunch on Degraves Street near Flinders Station and go from there...avoid main roads and keep your eyes open for things above or below ground, and never discount a dirty alleyway, you never know what you'll find—even if it is just some incredible street art.

Stores to visit would be the iconic establishment of Alice Euphemia—Karen Rieschieck's store has been an integral part of the Melbourne design scene since she opened in 1997 and she goes above and beyond to support young Australian design talent. Comeback Kid is also another awesome design store/space definitely worth a look-in.

ALICE EUPHEMIA
6, Cathedral Arcade
37 Swanston Street
Melbourne, Victoria
Australia
+61 (03) 9650 4300
WWW.ALICEEUPHEMIA.COM

COMEBACK KID
Level 1, 8 Rankins Lane
Melbourne, Victoria
+61 (03) 9670 7076
WWW.COMEBACKKID.COM.AU

For more on DI$COUNT visit
WWW.NODISCOUNT.COM.AU

DESIGNER DIRECTORY

ARNSDORF

Melbourne-based label gives classic garments modern cuts in crystaline shapes. **WWW.ARNSDORF.COM.AU**

COLLETTE DINNIGAN

The first Aussie designer to show at Paris Fashion Week, Collette Dinnigan is known for her ladylike garments. **WWW.COLLETTEDINNIGAN.COM.AU**

CHRONICLES OF NEVER

Former Ksubi designer Gareth Moody creates dark, unisex clothing. **WWW.CHRONICLESOFNEVER.COM**

DION LEE

Structured shapes with clean lines, crisp tailoring and clever cutouts. **WWW.DIONLEE.COM**

ELLERY

Exactly the type of clothing cool girls want to wear: fashion-forward, well constructed, and powerfully sexy. **WWW.ELLERYLAND.COM**

KIRRILY JOHNSTON

Global inspiration, Australian style. **WWW.KIRRILYJOHNSTON.COM**

KSUBI

All the essentials for a laidback look. **WWW.KSUBI.COM**

JOSH GOOT

Josh Goot shows in London, but his Australian roots are evident in his bright colors, beachy materials and short cuts. **WWW.JOSHGOOT.COM**

LOVER

Each collection starts with its own narrative (Patty Hearst, *Freaks and Geeks*), yet always retains a vintage-inspired, rock 'n' roll sensibility. **WWW.LOVERTHELABEL.COM**

ROMANCE WAS BORN

Imaginative styling and quirky details—watch-print pants, a sweater embellished with dollar bills—make Romance Was Born one of fashion's most exciting young labels. **WWW.ROMANCEWASBORN.COM**

COLETTE DINNIGAN

DION LEE

ELLERY

SASS & BIDE

After making a splash with low-slung denim, Sass & Bide expanded to luxurious clothing with a bit of an edge. **WWW.SASSANDBIDE.COM**

TONI MATICEVSKI

Toni Maticevski's floaty, feminine dresses have found a following on red carpets worldwide. **WWW.TONIMATICEVSKI.COM**

WE ARE HANDSOME

We Are Handsome's boldly printed one-piece swimsuits are handmade in limited editions. **WWW.WEAREHANDSOME.COM**

WILLOW

Kit Willow's feminine clothing features rich details, strong colors and references to nature. **WWW.WILLOWLTD.COM**

ZIMMERMANN

Nicole and Simone Zimmermann designed super-sexy swimwear before expanding to relaxed and sophisticated ready-to-wear in bold colors. **WWW.ZIMMERMANNWEAR.COM**

STORES

COLLETTE DINNIGAN
33 William Street
Paddington, NSW
+61 (02) 9360 6691

KIRRILY JOHNSTON
6 Glenmore Road
Paddington, NSW
+61 (02) 9380 7775

KSUBI
16 Glenmore Road
Paddington, NSW
+61 (02) 9361 6291

SASS & BIDE
132 Oxford Street
Paddington, NSW
+61 (02) 9360 3900

WILLOW
3A Glenmore Road
Paddington, NSW
+61 (02) 9358 4477

ROMANCE WAS BORN
FOR PANDORA

SASS
& BIDE

ZIMMERMANN

WE ARE HANDSOME

LOS ANGELES

1922 Sid Grauman introduces the red carpet at the premiere of *Robin Hood*

1966 Paul Van Doren makes sneaker history with Vans, his waffle-soled shoe

1960s Musicians like The Doors and Love take the bohemian
Laurel Canyon look worldwide

1980s Hair-metal style defines the Sunset Strip

1995 Cult classic film *Clueless* introduces the world to Beverly Hills style

1997 American Apparel sets up shop in Downtown L.A.

2003–2008 Mercedes-Benz hosts Los Angeles Fashion Week at Smashbox Studios

2009 BOXeight presents a three-day live photo shoot for L.A. Fashion Week

THE STYLE TRIBES OF L.A.

BY MAXWELL WILLIAMS

Time doesn't work in quite the same way in Southern California. Here, the alarm goes off a full three hours after New Yorkers are already busy and bustling around. It's the same with fashion. New Yorkers get themselves into a schvitz designing and sewing and fitting and modeling and styling and pricing and shipping. Later, a girl in Beverly Hills stretches her arms and heads on down to Rodeo Drive, noodles around in a couple stores, and ultimately comes out with a dozen bags and a brand-new look. That's not true of all Los Angeles fashion—there are plenty of amazing designers and stylists and photographers here. There just seems to be a sense that Los Angeles will let New York do all the work, and then poach the best parts and make it their own. In a city without seasons, time is kind to fashion. Things don't go out of fashion before they hit stores. Rather, style is divided by the geographically placed tribes of L.A. It is a journey of time and space quite unlike fashion of any other city in the world.

To fully understand this phenomenon, one needen't look farther than Sunset Junction, a small boutique-lined stretch of West Sunset Boulevard on the East Side of Los Angeles, where it's possible to meet up and have a Rwandan coffee at the café Intelligentsia before rummaging through vintage shops like Ozzie Dots and Squaresville. The purpose of this exercise, for many East Side dwellers, is to replicate the look

and feel of 1960s Laurel Canyon, which was, at the time, possibly the coolest place on earth. Laid-back folkie flower fashion ruled. Summer frocks and flowing sundresses and headbands matched sunshine-y vibes set to The Byrds' "Turn! Turn! Turn!" Jim Morrison made L.A. a denim suit town, while Frank Zappa and Arthur Lee of Love made it freak out with flower prints and boho layers. Somehow the sartorial debris all ended up in Silver Lake and Echo Park at the myriad thrift shops, to be found decades later by little hippie girls as pretty as their flower-power ancestors, and worn to The Echo, where bands like The

Growlers play Doors-like dirges. Then off to the school bus-sized dive just up the street, Little Joy, to quaff a cheap beer and have a good laugh.

But Los Angeles was not always about peace, love and all that shit. Recycling the fashions of late-'70s Hollywood punk—a style even scuzzier than that of New York or London—precocious hipster kids swarm to Downtown Los Angeles' The Smell. On any given night, the band onstage is sweaty and bare-chested, howling off-key to an off-kilter staccato beat. In the audience, a red-haired girl no older than 17 wears a homemade T-shirt spattered with red paint and a hand-painted scrawl that says, simply: "Your Mom After I'm Done With Her." The irony is layered thicker than the smog here. Los Angeles hipsters don't mess around.

The warehouse district, also in the Downtown area, is geared towards a population under the drinking age. Here lies the factory that churns out the current uniform of young Los Angeles hipsters: American Apparel. Despite their social platforms—A.A. are champions of social responsibility in the workplace, fair wages, and a staunch refusal to outsource most of their labor—American Apparel has a built a reputation

^ (TOP) AMERICAN APPAREL'S DOWNTOWN L.A. FACTORY
^ KICKING BACK AT FYF FESTIVAL, LOS ANGELES STATE HISTORIC PARK

for being a sexually questionable work environment, feeding fuel to the fire by holding "castings" for retail clerks and having their young employees model gold lamé leotards and throwback sweatbands and knee-highs while in sexually suggestive (read: porn-y) positions. The fact that notorious tailchaser Dov Charney heads the company only helps prove the point that Los Angeles doesn't really change. For, you see, sleazebags have long run Los Angeles' various industries, and here, sex always sells. American Apparel, now a worldwide brand doing millions upon millions of dollars in business, is built on a cheap-o type of aesthetic that has haunted Los Angeles fashion since the 1970s.

It all started when Southern California (and the San Fernando Valley in particular) became obsessed with pornography. Almost all U.S. porn is produced in Los Angeles, and it permeates into every facet of the city. It attracted a new species to California in the 1970s and 1980s: the douchebag. Now, though, they work in reality television or other types of media, they keep on coming. Just like Dov Charney marketed sexuality to young boys and girls, a man named Christian Audigier, who since 2004 has owned the Ed Hardy brand, figured out the exact kinds of threads this male demographic of Los Angeles desires. Walk into West Hollywood's Viper Room, Key Club or the Burbank Bar & Grille and there you'll find countless television executives and club owners—lured to Los Angeles by the promise of easy money and easier sex—getting down to David Guetta-produced

pop hits in crisp dragon-print dress shirts and tiger-embroidered hats, muscle-to-muscle at the bar, downing Red Bull and vodkas, and talking to their bros about sports. It may sound like a cartoon world, but it exists, all over Los Angeles.

The antithesis of the Ed Hardy/ Affliction/graffiti T-shirt crowd stands out in front of the old theaters of Hollywood, where a throng of rabid fans and paparazzi gather around a red carpet premiere as Gwyneth Paltrow struts around in her custom Valentino chiffon gown. Look, there's Brangelina—an Elie Saab dress, Cartier jewels, and Jimmy Choo shoes for her; Tom Ford or Dolce&Gabbana suit for him.

Totally suave, George Clooney turns and makes an on-camera joke in a Giorgio Armani two-piece, looking every bit a part of a decorous history as Douglas Fairbanks did when Sid Grauman rolled out Hollywood's first red carpet at his Egyptian Theatre for the *Robin Hood* premiere on October 18, 1922. Searchlights flooded the skies that night, drawing the attention of the entire world, changing the way we look at celebrity and fashion forever, spawning an industry of high fashion meant to be worn by the most demure actresses entering awards shows. Now, even CNN gets in on the "best and worst dressed" lists.

But celebrity alone can be boring and predictable (seriously, how many

^ (CLOCKWISE FROM LEFT) HOLLYWOOD NIGHTLIFE; KOURTNEY AND KIM KARDASHIAN PAPARAZZI GATHER TO SEE BRAD PITT AND ANGELINA JOLIE AT PREMIERE OF *INGLOURIOUS BASTERDS*

Tom Ford suits *are* there out there?). And in L.A., two men have perfectly melded celebrity and fashion culture with an almost Dali-esque sense of surrealism: Jeremy Scott and David LaChappelle. Both are friends to the stars; the former dressing them in his always eye-popping, sometimes bonkers, clothing, the latter putting them in plasticine scenarios and taking equally high-gloss photos. And on the other side of the same fame-driven spectrum are the starlets, the Lauren Conrads and Rachel Bilsons who fancy themselves designers.

It had to be mentioned—we *are* talking about Los Angeles after all—but we'll leave the rest of the celebrity talk to the tabloids. Instead, despite being a second-class city in American fashion, there is a burgeoning fashion community who are influenced not only by what came before, but the local environment. Take Trovata, for instance, the Ecco Domani-winning label based in Newport Beach. Their line takes the subtleties of the West Coast's surfer-town lifestyle and blends it with a more traditional East Coast preppy aesthetic. The result is a wonderfully wearable collection of knits and coats. Melissa Coker's Wren line blends bright California colors with ultra-femininity, while one of the most talked about up-and-coming menswear labels, Band of Outsiders, captures the blue-sportscoat-and-khakis look perfect for a poolside business meeting with your agent.

^ DAN OH FROM DIM MAK TUESDAYS IN DIM MAK COLLECTION

For those after a look that is more after-hours than Americana, Brian Lichtenberg's cheeky, oddball, drape-y style explores that quirky SoCal sense of humor through sexy party dresses and slack T-shirts. And while Grey Ant recently moved operations to New York, the label still crafts collections of strapless dresses and playful shirt-and-short combinations that look cool enough to wear to the club on a sweaty dance night, or light enough for a stroll down Venice Beach.

And of course, there are Los Angeles fashion's darling daughters, the Mulleavy sisters, head Pasadena-based label Rodarte, their critically-acclaimed line reflecting the California dream aesthetic with a bit of dark fashion sensibility thrown in for good measure. Los Angeles fashion design has come a long way from the days when Guess? Jeans and BCBGMAXAZRIA were the only players in town.

Still, there's more to fashion in Los Angeles. There's been a fashion week here since before Azria could say "bon chic, bon genre." It was called "Press Week" for a long time, and it was a citywide, scattered affair that no one really took seriously. Mercedes-Benz entered in 2002, teaming up with Smashbox Studios, and tried to legitimize Fashion Week

REQUIRED READING

FLAUNT
Cutting-edge art fashion, art and music. Each issue comes bundled with a limited-edition artwork. The team also throws some of the best parties in town. **WWW.FLAUNT.COM**

ANTHEM
It's all about emerging culture at *Anthem*, a quarterly with a focus on independent fashion, music film and more. **WWW.ANTHEM.COM**

BLEACH BLACK
Twin blog feeds track the musings of two fashionistas who share a love of the SoCal boho rocker look. **WWW.BLEACHBLACK.COM**

FASHIONTOAST
Love her or hate her, Rumi Neely has become one of the web's biggest—and most polarizing—fashion bloggers, landing a RVCA lookbook along the way. **WWW.FASHIONTOAST.COM**

WHO WHAT WEAR
Celeb style, runway looks and shopping deals. **WWW.WHOWHATWEAR.COM**

WHAT IS REALITY ANYWAY
Blogger Krystal Simpson's rock 'n' roll take on personal style.
WWW.WHATISREALITYANYWAY.COM

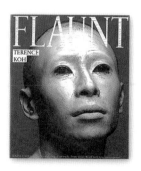

in L.A. by centralizing it. But in 2008, the relationship fell apart—the last presentation was a disaster—and Fashion Week has since had to survive without the backing of Mercedes. Local arts organization BOXeight began putting together worthy and creative shows in their large downtown studio space. The 2009 production featured a live photo shoot, open to the public: Viewers could mill about the back of the sets while the photographers worked. These unconventional flourishes have injected much needed energy into Fashion Week in Los Angeles. Side attractions such as the (sadly) defunct Gen Art's Avant Guardians and Fresh Faces programs and Downtown L.A. Fashion Week have made for an intriguing, if still scattered, Fashion Week. Despite a decentralized Fashion

Week, Los Angeles fashion has come a long way in the past few years. No longer are the archetypes of L.A. fashion surfer and skater labels like Quiksilver and Vans. Kids try out outrageous hipster styles at wild club nights at Cinespace, where Steve Aoki (brother of major fashion model Devon Aoki, and an heir of the Benihana restaurant fortune) has turned Dim Mak Records into the sovereign nation of the L.A. DJ scene, and party photographer Mark "The Cobra Snake" Hunter's camera captures it all. His former muse, teenybopper hipster icon Cory Kennedy, now appears regularly in magazines like *Nylon* and *teenVOGUE*. LA Models remains one of the top agencies in the world, attracting top stylists and photographers to the city. And small, cool labels are popping up

^ HAIR DESIGNER MICHAEL HAASE FROM UNITE AND GARRET GERVAIS
FROM DIOR BEAUTY WITH A MODEL AT BOXEIGHT STUDIOS

CELEB STYLE

Since opening in 2000, Kitson has become a symbol of a certain set of L.A. style. In the early aughts, the Robertson Boulevard boutique became a favorite of Young Hollywood starlets and celebutants—think Lindsay, Britney, Paris and their ilk. It also became a paparazzi hangout, and a regular feature in the tabloids press.

everywhere, like Corpus, Factory by Erik Hart, Orthodox, Skin.Graft and Fluxus by Jeffrey Sebelia, the latter headed by a *Project Runway* finalist. Gaudy is giving way to chic, asinine to austere.

Today the boutique still offers the pricey logo T-shirts, jeans and "It" bags that made it famous, as well as labels like the Kardashian Collection, Gwen Stefani's Harajuku Lovers and House of Harlow 1960, Nicole Richie's line of retro-inspired jewelry.

What L.A. needs is more risk-takers. The city is entrenched in an audacious style history. The hippie ethos, '80s Valley Girls, hair metal and skater culture all created a template for fashion here. Designers who embrace the combination of the dark sleaziness and the sunny brightness often succeed in creating interesting, L.A.-looking clothing. The high desert, the Pacific and the mountains create an inspirational terrain, giving designers and photographers and stylists something more to look at than New York's city streets and buildings. L.A.'s got style, and the world is beginning to take notice.

KITSON
115 S. Robertson Boulevard
Los Angeles, CA 90048
+1 310 859 2652

WWW.SHOPKITSON.COM

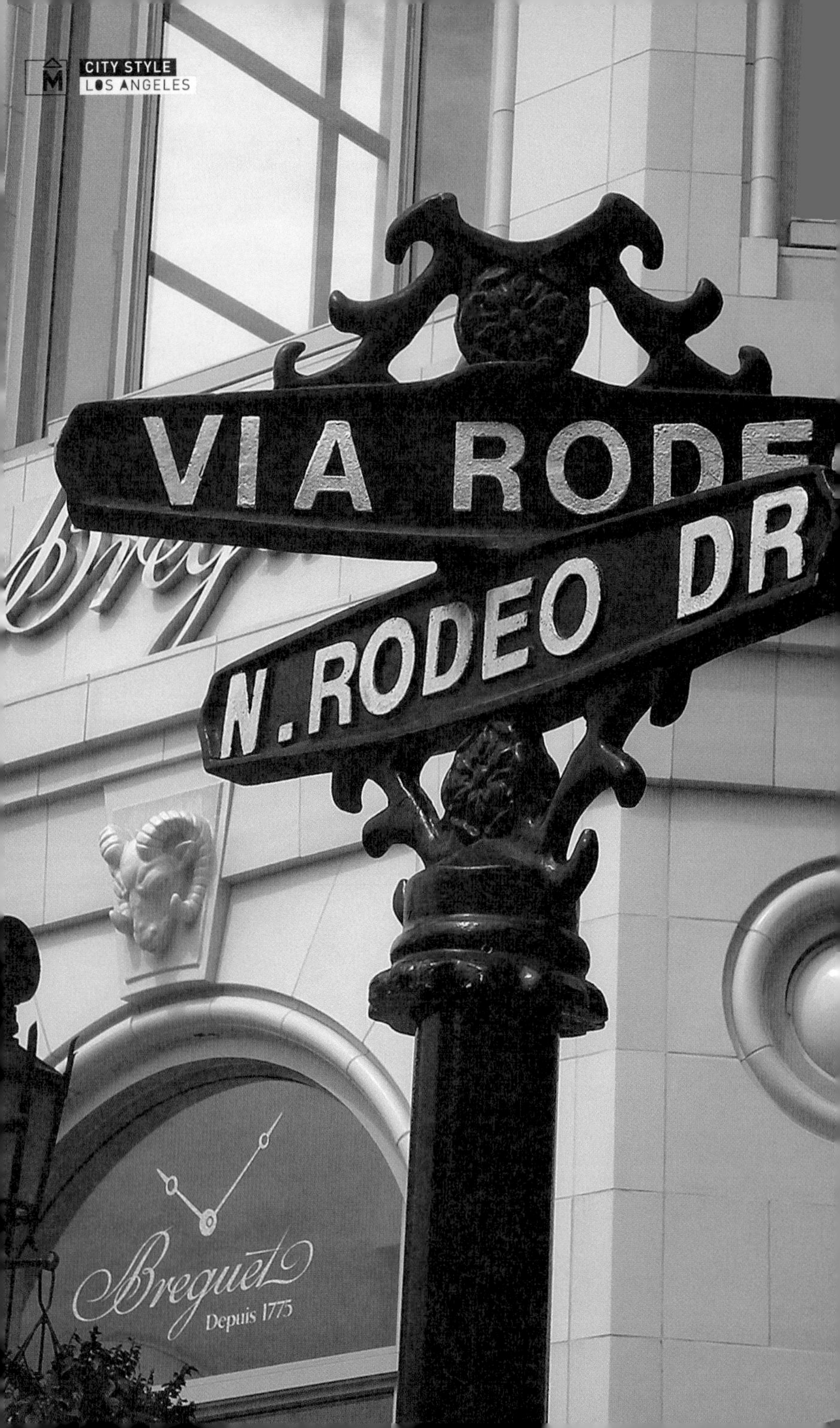

VIA RODE

N. RODEO DR

Breguet
Depuis 1775

NEIGHBORHOODS

BEVERLY HILLS
This glitzy city on the western edge of L.A. County is an international symbol of wealth and luxury.

DOWNTOWN
Gritty Downtown L.A. has seen a revival in the last decade with an influx of high-end hotels and businesses, including American Apparel.

EAST SIDE
Historically Hispanic, the East Side neighborhoods of Silver Lake, Echo Park and Los Feliz have become the core of young L.A. Here you'll find hip restaurants, bars and boutiques, plus a folky, rock 'n' roll look.

HOLLYWOOD
Hollywood is home to the movies and major tourist attractions, while its neighbor West Hollywood boasts the raucous clubs of the Sunset Strip and a sizeable gay community.

VENICE BEACH
It's all about a laid-back vibe in L.A.'s beautiful beach towns. For a more grown-up scene (and less tie-dye) try nearby Santa Monica.

< RODEO DRIVE, BEVERLY HILLS

HOTSPOTS

POLO LOUNGE
It's all about old-school Hollywood glamour at the Polo Lounge at the posh Beverly Hills Hotel. Come for a cocktail, brunch or tea, and stay for the people watching.

9641 Sunset Boulevard
Beverly Hills, California
+1 310 276 2251
WWW.BEVERLYHILLSHOTEL.COM

CHATEAU MARMONT
This West Hollywood hideaway has been a favorite of rock stars and celebs—and the scene of some serious mischief since the 1930s.

8221 Sunset Boulevard
Hollywood, California
+1 323 656 1010
WWW.CHATEAUMARMONT.COM

TROUSDALE
The L.A. club scene is always on the lookout for the next big thing, and for a moment, ultra-lounge Trousdale is the place to be. In a city that loves an exclusive club, this newcomer offers a velvet rope that's hard to get past. Once inside revelers find danceable beats and sleek décor, from the people behind former hotspot Hyde.

9229 Sunset Boulevard
West Hollywood, California
+1 310 274 7500

SOHO HOUSE WEST HOLLYWOOD
L.A.'s branch of private club Soho House is a favorite with celebs and schmoozers.

9200 Sunset Boulevard
West Hollywood, California
+1 310 432 9200
WWW.SOHOHOUSEWH.COM

< THE POOL AT CHATEAU MARMONT

KING COBRA
MARK HUNTER

Mark Hunter became famous for taking photos of California cool kids and posting them to his website, The Cobra Snake. Since the site launched in 2003, Hunter has become something of a cultural icon, while The Cobra Snake remains the go-to place for a certain type of gritty, barely-legal hipster style.

Hunter describes himself as a "nice Jewish boy," and for someone who's found so much success, so young, he actually is a really nice guy. (During this interview, he put us on hold to ask his grandparents if he could borrow the car.) His job description includes party-hopping around the globe, but Hunter always comes back to the West Hollywood bungalow he calls home.

^ DESIGNER KARL LAGERFELD WITH MARK HUNTER

Hi Mark, could you introduce yourself?
My name is Mark and there's a website called The Cobra Snake where I travel around the world taking pictures of pretty much everything from fashion shows to music festivals to underground warehouse parties and art shows and bar mitzvahs and birthday parties and weddings. I post everything to the website, where you can look for fashion inspiration and learn about new music that you'll like, and just discover this awesome world of creative people.

HOW WOULD YOU DESCRIBE L.A. STYLE?
It's a little more casual than other places, not so serious. It's California—we always have nice weather—so we don't have to really worry too much about heavy layering and stuff like that. On one hand, we don't get all those fun fashion accessories as much as New York, or European places that get below zero, but we work on what we have.

IS THERE AN OFFICIAL L.A. LOOK?
I'd say simple jeans and a T-shirt, or cut-off

shorts and a T-shirt for girls. Nice shoes and a nice bag make anything work.

WHERE CAN YOU GET THE LOOK?
I have my own shop, the Cobra Shop, by appointment only, in L.A. I have my own line coming out, but besides that we carry vintage that I hand-select from all around the world. It's basically the kind of things you see in the photos on my website, you can buy in real life. I like Jet Rag and Opening Ceremony and Confederacy, and if you can get a private appointment with Jeremy Scott, he lives here.

TELL ME ABOUT YOUR LINE.
It's very surf-skate inspired, I'm doing

it with this company RVCA. They did a line with Erin Wasson that's been pretty successful over the past few seasons. It's basically clothes that I like, and that I want to wear and then I got to make them. They're kind of loud, and out there, and a bit eccentric like I am. It's a little unisex, which is instant cool for anyone that's looking to be cool.

WHEN IT COMES TO STYLE, HOW DOES L.A. STACK UP AGAINST OTHER CITIES?
It's not the most stylish. L.A. in general doesn't try too hard. With all these fashion snapper blogs, you go to New York during Fashion Week—or even not fashion week—or you go to Paris anytime, there's

^ MARK HUNTER AND TWO OF HIS DESIGNS FOR RVCA

some serious people that are obsessed with that kind of stuff. It's not as much in L.A. I give it like a 7 out of 10, or something.

YOUR SITE GOES BACK BEFORE THE WHOLE STREET STYLE THING BLEW UP ON THE WEB.
Hell, yeah.

WHAT DO YOU THINK ABOUT IT?
I'm surprised that there's such a market. Especially outside of the fashion shows, you'll see like 30 bloggers that are there taking street style photos and somehow they're making a living doing the exact same thing, taking pictures of the exact same people. I find that kind of funny. I'm glad that they're doing that and they're a

bit liberated from working for the man. I support anybody's form of creativity, however original or not original it is.

DO YOU HAVE ANY TIPS FOR SOMEONE HOPING TO END UP ON A SITE LIKE YOURS...HOW TO CATCH YOUR EYE?
I try to capture people really having fun and not trying too hard or anything. When you can be natural and free-spirited and stylish and cool and not over-the-top. Anything over-the-top is a little bit too much; it's too obnoxious.

Visit Mark at **WWW.THECOBRASNAKE.COM**

VINTAGE CHIC
CAMERON SILVER

When Hollywood's A-list needs a one-of-a-kind garment for that special event, they go to Cameron Silver. As the owner of Decades and Decadestwo, two high-end boutiques specializing in the crème de la crème of designer vintage, Silver is the man who put Chloë Sevigny in Thierry Mugler, dressed

Gwyneth Paltrow in Christian Dior, and brought vintage back in style.

IN YOUR OWN WORDS, HOW WOULD YOU DESCRIBE DECADES?

Decades is a purveyor of collectible 20th-century vintage couture in a friendly and elegant setting.

YOU SPECIALIZE IN A CERTAIN TYPE OF HOLLYWOOD GLAMOUR. HOW WOULD YOU DESCRIBE THE "DECADES LOOK?"
It's all about vintage that looks modern... never boring and never basic.

HOW DO YOU FIND SO MANY AMAZING PIECES?
We find the best things coming out of closets of "women of a certain age" with great style.

SO MANY STARS TURN TO YOU FOR RED CAR-PET WORTHY LOOKS. HOW WOULD YOU DEFINE HOLLYWOOD STYLE?

Hollywood vintage red-carpet glamour is all about the memorable moment when a celebrity is photographed in something that is mysterious, timeless and iconic.

WHAT SHOULD BUYERS LOOK FOR WHEN INVESTING IN A VINTAGE PIECE?
Quality is paramount along with form and function that doesn't look anachronistic.

WHAT ELEMENTS CONTRIBUTE TO A TIMELESS LOOK/HELP A GARMENT STAND THE TEST OF TIME?
When purchasing vintage, ask yourself,

"Does this look modern?" If you follow this suggestion you will buy vintage that doesn't look costume-y.

WHAT ARE THE KEYS TO KEEPING VINTAGE IN GOOD SHAPE OVER THE YEARS?
Protect your vintage from the elements and these garments, which are better made than today's mass-produced contemporary pieces, should last a long time.

YOU OBVIOUSLY KNOW A THING OR TWO ABOUT THE GOOD LIFE. WHAT ARE YOUR FAVORITE CHIC HANGOUTS IN LOS ANGELES?

I like iconic clothes and iconic restaurants: Polo Lounge, Musso & Frank, La Scala, El Coyote and my home!

DECADES
8214 ½ Melrose Ave
Los Angeles, California
+1 323 655 0223

For more information, or to check out the Daily Arrival Blog visit **WWW.DECADESINC.COM**

PASADENA

The SoCal city of Pasadena—a northern neighbor of Los Angeles—is the unlikely homebase of two of fashion's biggest names, Kate and Laura Mulleavy of Rodarte. The label's recent collections have found inspiration from the side of the 110 Freeway (the main drag connecting Pasadena to Los Angeles) and in Texas border towns, far away from the fashion fray in New York, where the label is shown.

But long before the Mulleavy's started making clothes out of the parents' house, the fashion set came to Pasadena for a different reason—the Rose Bowl Flea Market. A vintage lover's dream, the Rose Bowl Flea Market features over 2,500 vendors on the second Sunday of each month, when more than 20,000 shoppers descend on the city.

Admission is $8 at 9 a.m., but savvy shoppers know to get there early. Arrive between 5 and 7 a.m. and admission will set you back $20, a small price to pay for first dibs on the goods.

For more information visit: **WWW.RGCSHOWS.COM**

^ THE ROSE BOWL FLEA MARKET, PASADENA

RODARTE

It's amazing how far Kate and Laura Mulleavy's Rodarte label has come since its 2005 inception. With no formal fashion training, the Pasadena natives have captivated the fashion elite with their borderline-obsessive attention to detail and uncanny ability to capture the ephemeral in their dresses.

Soft lines and experimentation with fabric have been the mainstays of the label since the beginning, but their simple cocktail dresses and romantic suits have given way to complete immersion in concept and a more aggressive point of view.

Their signature loose, multi-color knits first made an appearance in 2008 and soon after they began utilizing those techniques with different materials; within a year they were creating clothes that were essentially beautifully woven fabric collages. Their designs walk a fine line between haute couture and ready-to-wear, and though their price point is definitely not accessible to the masses, their influence is felt in all corners of the market.

With collaborations with Gap and Target under their belt, it seems the sky's the limit for the sisters who make dresses out of dreams.

For more information on Rodarte
VISIT WWW.RODARTE.NET

BAND OF OUTSIDERS

Scott Sternberg's smart interpretations of classic pieces—khakis, blazers and trench coats—have earned a cult following for Band of Outsiders and sister label Boy. **WWW.BANDOFOUTSIDERS.COM**

BCBGMAXAZRIA

With six lines to his name, Max Azria keeps busy designing dresses for young Hollywood. **WWW.BCBG.COM**

BRAIN LICHTENBERG

Brain Lichtenberg's body-con dresses, slouchy Ts, tanks and bold graphic jewelry are ready for a night at the club. **WWW.BRIANLICHTENBERG.COM**

CORPUS

A masculine line of tailored denim that evolved into a full-fledged sportswear label. Their Urban Outfitters collaboration byCORPUS features a pretty-preppy sensibility. **CORPUSCLOTHING.COM**

ERIK HART

The designer behind Factory, Morphine Generation and the Urban Outfitters collab Dark Harts, Erik Hart is a musician and it shows. Even his most feminine designs feature a rough, rock 'n' roll edge. **WWW.FACTORYCOLLECTION.COM**

FLUXUS

Project Runway alum Jeffrey Sebelia recently took the reins at Fluxus, a label known for soft and cozy separate pieces. **WWW.FLUXUSBRAND.COM**

GABBY APPLEGATE

Formerly known as Witches, Gabby Applegate's signature label features dark and drapey clothing. **WWW.GABBYAPPLEGATE.COM**

GOLDSPUN

Specializing in Japanese demin, Goldspun creates updated versions of classic pieces. **WWW.GOLDSPUN07.COM**

JEREMY SCOTT

Jeremy Scott is fashion's Pop Art master, refrencing everything from the Flintstones to American Express, while artfully blurring the line between the lowbrow and high fashion. **JEREMYSCOTT.COM**

BOY
BY BAND OF OUTSIDERS

BRIAN
LICHTENBERG

ISABEL
LU

ISABEL LU

Sophia Kim creates simple, silky garments with lots of sex appeal. **ISABELLU.COM**

LE SANG DES BETES

Film, architecture and sculpture inspire Trang Chau's modern-gothic designs.
WWW.LESANGDESBETES.COM

LNA

All the stretchy basics needed for a well-rounded wardrobe with a bit of edge. **LNA.COM**

ORTHODOX

Modern, with a hint of tradition, Orthodox makes sophisticated clothes for grown-up surfer dudes.
ORTHODOXCLOTHING.COM

RAQUEL ALLEGRA

Raquel Allegra's shredded garments have often been copied, but few can recreate her super-soft feel. Allegra reworks worn-out Ts from the L.A. County Jail, for a local take on recycling.
WWW.RAQUELALLEGRA.COM

RVCA

Sunny SoCal style, surfing and skateboarding, plus collabs with the likes of model Erin Wasson and the Artist Network Program. **WWW.RVCA.COM**

SKIN.GRAFT

Dark designs with a vintage vibe and structured leather.
SKINGRAFTDESIGNS.COM

TROVATA

East Coast prep meets laid-back West Coast style.
WWW.TROVATA.COM

WREN

Classic American staples with a ladylike finish. A favorite of Alexa Chung, Filippa Berg and other icons of the girly style set.
WWW.WREN-CLOTHING.COM

STORES

BCBGMAXAZRIA
443 North Rodeo Drive
Beverly Hills, California
+1 310 275 3024

FLUXUS
202 North Larchmont
Los Angeles, California
+1 323 465 9339

SKIN.GRAFT
125 West 4th Street #102
Los Angeles, California
+1 213 626 2662

RVCA / VALA
501 North Fairfax Avenue
Los Angeles, California
+1 323 951 0901

TROVATA
505 31st Street
Newport Beach, California
+1 949 675 5904

JEREMY SCOTT

RAQUEL ALLEGRA

WREN

INDEX

INDEX

INDEX

PHOTO CREDITS

CONTENTS

New York: © Akira Chiba; Paris: © Heather Corcoran; Milan: Courtesy of February; London: © Iain McKell; Tokyo: Courtesy of Swagger; Stockholm: Courtesy of Filippa K; Sydney: © Nelson Bernard; L.A.: © Derek Purdy

CONTRIBUTORS

New York: Courtesy of Laia Garcia; Milan: Fabiana Fierotti © Leandro J. Richman, Ilaria Norsa © Lady Tarin; Tokyo: Courtesy of Dan Bailey; London: Jem Goudling © Nacho Alegre; Paris: Lauren Drablier © Heather Corcoran; Stockholm: Courtesy of Andy Carlson; Sydney: Courtesy of Paul Bui; LA: Maxwell William © Hiroki Kobayashi

NEW YORK

10: © Akira Chiba; 12-13: (top) Fashion Week © Kei Kondo, (bottom) © Michael Moran; 14: (top) © Akira Chiba, (bottom) Courtesy of Sophomore; 15: Courtesy of The Metropolitan Museum of Art; 16: Courtesy of Opening Ceremony; 17-19 © Akira Chiba; 20: (left) © Akira Chiba, (right) © Matthew Sussman; 21: © Mat Szwajkos Courtesy of Steven Alan; 22 (bottom left) Courtesy of Zero + Maria Cornejo; 22-27 © Akira Chiba; 28-31 Courtesy of Vena Cava, designer portrait © Georgia Nerheim; 32-35: © Eddie Newton; 38: Courtesy of Calvin Klein/©Dan Lecca, Photo by Slaven Vlasic/Getty Images for Mercedes-Benz; 39: Courtesy of Marc Jacobs/© Dan and Corina Lecca, Photo by Fernanda Calfat/Getty Images for Mercedes-Benz; 40: Courtesy of Anna Sui/©Thomas Lau, Photo by Frazer Harrison/Getty Images for Mercedes-Benz, Photo by Frazer Harrison/Getty Images for Mercedes-Benz; 41: Photo by Frazer Harrison/Getty Images for Mercedes-Benz, Courtesy of Oscar de la Renta, Jemal Countess/Getty Images for Mercedes-Benz; 42: Frazer Harrison/Getty Images for Mercedes-Benz, Courtesy of Alexander Wang , Courtesy of Jason Wu; 43: Courtesy of Ohne Titel/©Amy Troost, Courtesy of Thakoon, Coutesy of Vena Cava; 44: Courtesy of Jen Kao, Courtesy of Katie Gallagher; 45: Courtesy of Sophomore, Courtesy of Tim Hamilton, Courtesy of Zero + Maria Cornejo

PARIS

46-62: © Heather Corcoran; 63: Courtesy of Colette; 64: © Max Abadian 65: Courtesy of Rad Hourani; 66-67: © Heather Corcoran; 68-69: © Gildas Paraiso; 71 Courtesy of A.F. Vandevorst/© Etienne Tordoir; 73: Courtesy of Walter Van Beirendonck / © Dan Lecca; 74-75 © Chris Moore/Catwalking, © Karl Prouse/Catwalking, © Chris Moore/Catwalking, © Chris Moore/Catwalking; 76: Courtesy of Chloé, Courtesy of Kenzo, 78: Courtesy of Damir Doma, Courtesy of Gaspard Yurkievich, Courtesy of Maison Martin Margiela, 79: Courtesy of Martin Grant, Courtesy of Rick Owens, Courtesy of Viktor & Rolf; 80: Courtesy of Heimstone; Courtesy of Paul & Joe; Page 81 Courtesy of The Kooples, Courtesy of Zadig & Voltaire

MILAN

81-84: © Heather Corcoran; 85: Courtesy of FEBRUARY; 86-92: © Heather Corcoran; 88: Courtesy of PIG magazine; 93-94: Courtesy of Fabiana Fierotti; 95: © Matteo Montanari; 96-97: Courtesy of Fabiana Fierotti; 98-99: © Heather Corcoran; 102-103: Courtesy of Bulgari; 104-106 © Tamu McPherson; 108: Courtesy of Gucci, Courtesy of Giorgio Armani; 109: Courtesy of Prada, Courtesy of Valentino; 110: Courtesy of Blumarine, Courtesy of Diesel, Courtesy of DSquared2; 111: Courtesy of Etro, Courtesy of Roberto Cavalli, Courtesy of Salvatore Ferragamo

LONDON

112: © Tom Beard; 114-117: © Jem Goulding, 118: (left) Courtesy of Liberty London; 119: © Nacho Alegre; 120: Courtesy of Elliot Atkinson; 121: © Susanna Lau; 122-123: © Iain McKell; 125-127: © Jem Goulding; 128-129: Courtesy of The Institute of Contemporary Arts; 130-131: Courtesy of Danielle Scutt; 132-135: Courtesy of Christopher Shannon; 136: Courtesy of Alexander McQueen, Courtesy of Burberry; 137: © Nathalie Lagneau/Catwalking, Courtesy of Vivienne Westwood; 138: Courtesy of Hussein Chalayan, Courtesy of

Jonathan Saunders; 139: Courtesy of Matthew Williamson; Courtesy of Sophia Kokosalaki; 140: Courtesy of Basso & Brooke, Courtesy of Erdem; 141: Courtesy of Kinder Aggugini; Courtesy of Richard Nicoll; 142: Courtesy of Felder Felder, Courtesy of Holly Fulton, Courtesy of Krystof Strozyna; 143: Courtesy of Louise Gray, Courtesy of Mark Fast, Courtesy of William Tempest

TOKYO

144: Courtesy of Swagger; 146-147: Courtesy of Dan Bailey/www.tokyodandy.com; 148: © Misaki Matsui; 149: Courtesy of Shibuya109; 150: Courtesy of DRESSEDUNDRESSED; 162: Courtesy of Laforet; 162-163 © Jimmy Cohrssen; 154: Courtesy of Phenomenon; 156: Courtesy of A Bathing Ape; 157: Courtesy of Dan Bailey/www.tokyodandy.com; 158-159: Courtesy of Maniac Corporation; 161: Courtesy of Dan Bailey/www.tokyodandy.com; 162-163: Courtesy of Baby Mary/Faline; 164-165: Courtesy of Daisuke Yakota/www.dropsnap.jp; 166-169: Courtesy of Toga; 170: Courtesy of ISSEY MIYAKE, Credit COMME des GARÇONS 2010-11 A / W; 171: Courtesy of Yohji Yamamoto/©Monica Feudi, Courtesy of Limi Feu; 172: Courtesy of Candy, Courtesy of Maniac Corporation, Courtesy of Fur Fur; 173: Courtesy of G.V.G.V., Courtesy of Dress Camp, Courtesy of Grimoire; Courtesy of Mister Hollywood, Courtesy of Milk, Courtesy of Sister; 174: Courtesy of Swagger, Courtesy of Galaxxxy, Courtesy of Phenomenon/©Hiroyuki Kamo

STOCKHOLM

176: Courtesy of Fifth Avenue Shoe Repair, 178-179 © Melanie Magassa; 180: Courtesy of Filippa K; 181 Courtesy of H&M; 182: Courtesy of Filippa K; 183: Courtesy of Fifth Avenue Shoe Repair; 184: Courtesy of Nordiska Kompaniet / © Elisabeth Ohlson Wallin; 185: Courtesy Nordiska Kompaniet / © Kristian Löveborg; 186-193: © Melanie Magassa; 194: Courtesy of Filipa Berg; 196: Courtesy of Cheap Monday; 197: Courtesy of Wood Wood/Agency V; 198: Courtesy of Copenhagen Fashion Week Photos by: Emile Sadria; 199: Courtesy of Wood Wood/Agency V, Courtesy of Stine Goya/Agency V, Courtesy of Henrik Vibskov/Agency V; 200: Courtesy of Acne, Courtesy of Ann-Sofie Back/© Tim Griffiths, Courtesy of Carin Wester; 201: Courtesy of Cheap Monday, Courtesy of Filippa K, Courtesy of Hope

SYDNEY

202: © Nelson Bernard; 204-205: © Byron Spencer; 206: (left) Courtesy of Oyster, (right) © Nelson Bernard; 208-209: © Nelson Bernard; 210: Courtesy of Zimmermann; 211-214: © Byron Spencer; 215: Courtesy of Love; 216-217: Courtesy of Belinda; 218-219: © Bryon Spencer; 220-221: Courtesy of Willow; 222-226: Courtesy of DI$COUNT; 228: Courtesy of Colette Dinnigan, Courtesy of Dion Lee, Courtesy of Ellery; 229: Courtesy of Romance Was Born; Courtesy Sass & Bide, Courtesy of Zimmerman; 230-231: Courtesy of We Are Handsome/Photographer: Sebastian Kriete/Designer: Jeremy Somers/www.wearehandsome.com

LOS ANGELES

232: Courtesy of Band of Outsiders/©Akira Yamada, 235: (clockwise from top left) © Alan Light, Courtesy of Fred Segal, © Derek Purdy; 236: (top) Courtesy of American Apparel, (bottom) © Drury Brennan; 237: Courtesy of American Apparel; 238: © (left and top) Drury Brennan, (bottom) Tzuu-Wang Shein; 239: Courtesy of Travota; 240: Courtesy of Dim Mak/© Quang Le; 241: Courtesy of Flaunt Magazine; 242: © Chad Wilson; 243: (left) Courtesy of Band of Outsiders/©Akira Yamada, (right) Courtesy of Kitson; 244-245: © Alberto Graci; 246-247: Courtesy of Chateau Marmont/© Nikolas Koenig; 248-251: Courtesy of Mark Hunter, 252-255: Courtesy of Decades; © Courtesy of R.G. Canning Enterprises; 257: © Tavi Gevinsen; 258: Courtesy of Band of Outsiders/© Akira Yamada, Courtesy of Brian Lichtenberg/www.alexandchloe.com, Courtesy of BOXeight/©Adam Secore; 259: Courtesy of Jeremy Scott, Courtesy of Raquel Allegra, Courtesy of Trovata, Courtesy of Wren; 260-261: Courtesy of Band of Outsiders/© Akira Yamada.

BIBLIOGRAPHY

Frankel, Susannah. *Visionaries: Interviews with Fashion Designers*, V&A Publishing, London, 2001
Godoy, Tiffany. *Style Deficit Disorder: Harajuku Street Fashion*, Tokyo, Chronicle Books, San Francisco, 2007
Jaeger, Anne-Celine. *Fashion Makers, Fashion Shapers*, Thames & Hudson, New York, 2009
Stanfill, Sonnett. *New York Fashion*, V&A Publishing, London, 2007

ACKNOWLEDGEMENTS

In addition to our writers, Museyon would like to thank the many people–from PR reps to photographers–who helped in the creation of this book, especially:

NEW YORK
Sophie Buhai
Kei Kondo
Jennifer Mankins
Lisa Mayock
Eddie Newton
Hannah Rood

PARIS
Rad Hourani
Kristopher Houser
Maggie Hunter
Kris Neko
Olof Norelid
Maroussia Rebecq
Guillaume Salmon
Jessica Schein

MILAN
Claus Breinholt
Marco Ceccato
Tamu McPherson
Jakob Thau
Francesco Tremolada

LONDON
Nacho Alegre (www.nachoalegre.com)
Tom Beard
Graeme Gaughan
Kerry Haynes

Danielle Scutt
Christopher Shannon
Steve Walsh

TOKYO
Baby Mary
Yasuko Furuta
Tatsuya Kanamori
Daisuke Yokota (www.dropsnap.jp)

STOCKHOLM
Filippa Berg
Rike Döpp/Agency V
Rachel B. Doyle
Melanie Magassa
(www.melaniemagassa.com)

SYDNEY
Nelson Bernard
Libby Haan
Cami James
Nadia Napreychikov
Byron Spencer
Kit Willow

L.A.
Drury Brennan
Tavi Gevinson (www.thestylerookie.com)
Mark Hunter (www.thecobrasanke.com)
Cameron Silver

MUSEYON, INC.

Publisher: Akira Chiba
Editor-in-Chief: Heather Corcoran
Media Editor: Jennifer Kellas
Editorial Consultant: Anne Ishii
Sales and Marketing Manager: Laura Robinson

Art Director: Ray Yuen
Cover Illustration: Jean-Philippe Delhomme
Cover Design: Bianca BeeZee Zvorc
Photo Researcher: Misaki Matsui
Proofreader: Mackenzie Allison, Tyler Seeger

MUSEYON GUIDES
A Curated Guide to Your Obsessions

CHRONICLES OF OLD NEW YORK
Exploring Manhattan's Landmark Neighborhoods

The history of NYC is written in its streets; discover 400 years of innovation through the true stories of the visionaries, risk-takers, dreamers, and schemers who built Manhattan with *Chronicles of Old New York*. Witness life in the city, when Greenwich Village was a bucolic suburb and disease was a fact of daily life. Find out which park covers a sea of unmarked graves. Explore the city's dark side, from the slums of Five Points to Harlem's Prohibition-era speakeasies. Then see it all for yourself with guided walking tours of each of Manhattan's historic neighborhoods.

ART + TRAVEL EUROPE
Step Into the Lives of Five Famous Painters

Van Gogh. Munch. Vermeer. Caravaggio. Goya. Five iconic artists whose inspirational works have been obsessed over by art lovers and travelers for years. To see masterpieces such as *Starry Night* and *The Scream* up close is awe-inspiring, but we know true devotees want even more. So we're taking you to where many of these artists' works were created in the places they lived, loved, and labored. To truly understand a man you must walk a few miles in his footsteps.

MUSIC + TRAVEL WORLDWIDE
Touring the Globe through Sounds and Scenes

With this new guidebook, curated by experts in the industry, you will: travel to Russia and experience the country's long and inglorious outlaw culture's sounds of chanson; go "underground" to check out Beijing's ever-evolving, experimental music scene; and get into Berlin's private clubs that are playing the offspring of techno. With 12 genres and influences, cities and scenes, *Music + Travel Worldwide* guides you across an insightful, international stage of sounds that helps you plan where to go and figure out what not to miss.

Pick up all of the Museyon Guides and follow your obsessions all over the world.

FILM + TRAVEL EUROPE
Traveling the World Through Your Favorite Movies

Visit Almeria, Spain and be transported into the iconic scenes of *Lawrence of Arabia*. Enjoy an incredible view of Paris from *Amélie's* Montmartre. Mail a postcard in Procida, Italy and see the sights shot in *Il Postino*. Prowl through the neighborhoods of Hamburg like Dennis Hopper and feel the eerie glow that is emitted in *The American Friend*. Find out how the location of *Atonement* was found and why Iceland stood in for the sands of Iwo Jima, and much more.

FILM + TRAVEL N. AMERICA, S. AMERICA
Traveling the World Through Your Favorite Movies

Report a fire at the Hook & Ladder Company #8 at *Ghostbusters'* headquarters in New York City. In San Francisco, stop for a cup of coffee at the café where Steve McQueen's *Bullit* meets an informant. Bring your own box of chocolates to Chippewa Square, Savannah and reenact the iconic scenes from *Forrest Gump*. Visit the Marine Building in Vancouver and be transported to Clark Kent's employer, The Daily Planet, in *Smallville*. Find out what part of Puerto Rico posed for *The Lord of the Flies*, why Madonna evaded Argentina when playing Eva Peron, and much more.

FILM + TRAVEL ASIA, OCEANIA, AFRICA
Traveling the World Through Your Favorite Movies

Drive into the parking garage at the University of Melbourne and follow in the footsteps of *Mad Max*. Whisper your deepest desires into the walls of Ta Prom Temple in Cambodia and recreate *In the Mood For Love*. Warm up your vocal chords at Karaoke-kan in Tokyo and pay homage to *Lost in Translation*. Discover which tiny Tasmanian town of 300 residents inspires Hayao Miyazaki, the anime mastermind behind *Spirited Away* and *Kiki's Delivery Service*. Find out when the scenery of Vietnam is in Cambodia and when it's in Puerto Rico and much more.

MUSEYON
GUIDES

ABOUT MUSEYON

Named after the Museion, the ancient Egyptian institute dedicated to the muses, Museyon Guides is an independent publisher that explores the world through the lens of cultural obsessions. Intended for frequent fliers and armchair travelers alike, our books are expert-curated and carefully researched, offering rich visuals, practical tips, and quality information.

Pick one up and follow your interests... wherever they might go.